D1572477

Reincarnation Cards®

AWAKENING FAR MEMORY

John M. Knowles, M.A.
Linda Leblanc

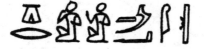

PAPHOS, CYPRUS 2007

Ger Maa Publishers
(Member of the Psychognosis Group)
P.O. Box 62064, 8060 Paphos, Cyprus (CY)
www.reincarnationcards.com
Email: info@reincarnationcards.com

Boxed set	ISBN-10: 9963-667-00-7	ISBN-13: 978-9963-667-00-0
Book	ISBN-10: 9963-667-02-3	ISBN-13: 978-9963-667-02-4

Card illustration and design: Patricia Peters ~ Book and box design: Janice M. Phelps
Reincarnation Cards® is a registered trademark of John M. Knowles and Linda Leblanc.
Eckhart Tolle's quote from *Stillness Speaks* used with permission of New World Library

PRINTED IN CHINA

SECOND IMPRESSION 2008

Disclaimer: The purpose of this project is both to entertain and to educate. The
authors and Ger Maa Publishers shall have neither liability for nor responsibility
to any person or entity with respect to any loss or damage caused, or alleged to
have been caused, directly or indirectly, by the information contained in this
book-cum-card set.

Dedication

This work is lovingly dedicated to the seers and sages of East and West, ancient and modern, whose insight has penetrated the ultimate mysteries of life and death and who, without thought of reward, freely *gave* of their knowledge to humankind. It is especially dedicated to the memory of those countless realized philosophers who, untold ages ago, illuminated the prehistoric world with their wisdom but whose names and very existence have been lost to us, and who must remain forever unknown.

"I should not wonder, indeed, if Euripides is right when he says: 'Who knoweth if to live is to be dead, and to be dead is to live?' And one might wonder if we are all really dead, and the body is our tomb. . ."

Iamblichus 250–330 CE

Acknowledgments

We are deeply indebted to all of the authors who are listed in the Bibliography and to countless others from whose labors we have benefited over the many years during which we have accumulated a research library that is surely unique in the eastern Mediterranean and Middle East area. We have, moreover, been particularly helped by our personal acquaintance with such luminaries as John Anthony West, co-discoverer after Schwaller de Lubicz of the erosion by water of the Egyptian Sphinx, which with the support of another acquaintance, the geologist Dr. Robert Schoch, has convincingly overthrown the conventional wisdom concerning its age. We have also met with Robert Bauval, Graham Hancock, Michael Baigent, the late Barry Fell, and other great investigators into humankind's lost pre- and protohistory.

Our philosophical approach owes much to the ancients such as Lao Tze, Ashtavakra, Gaudapada, Shankara, and that great modern sage, the late Paul Brunton, who in the last century was enormously instrumental in bringing the best of Indian philosophy to Western readers.

No project of the magnitude of this work could possibly have been brought to fruition by two people working in isolation in a remote corner of the Mediterranean world without outside help. This was provided by our extremely competent book shepherd, Janice Marie Phelps, of Lancaster, Ohio, who has guided its development throughout. We are also deeply indebted to our long-time friend, the peerless artist Patricia Peters, of Lovingston, Virginia, who prepared all of the *Reincarnation Cards*® from the initial sketches required for our patent applications, through to the final artwork. We are particularly grateful for the encouragement received to write on philosophy by such eminent thinkers as the late Paul Brunton and Arthur Ellison, as well as Stanley Krippner who has been so generous as to write the Foreword to this book.

✖ ✖ ✖

Table of Contents

"Reincarnation doesn't help you if in your next incarnation you still don't know who you are."

Eckhart Tolle, Stillness Speaks

*"Behold, now is the accepted time.
Behold, now is the day of salvation."*

St. Paul (II Corinthians 6.2)

Foreword

STANLEY KRIPPNER, PH.D.

The literary market is replete with Tarot and other card sets of various kinds, designed to tell fortunes, or to entertain or to assist users, in some sense, to accelerate their spiritual or psychological development. Given the number and variety of such sets, coupled with the popularity of the subject of reincarnation, it is surprising that nothing quite comparable to *Reincarnation Cards®* — *Awakening Far Memory* has ever been attempted.

The discerning reader may note its conceptual similarity to various projective personality tests used in psychology. These cards have much in common with, for example, the Thematic Apperception Test, involving responses to pictures and, especially, the Rorschach Inkblot Test, a device designed to evoke responses from the subject's unconscious that are alleged to reveal someone's personality dynamics. These technologies are not always productive, but when they are helpful they represent the positive effects of attribution, projection, and association. When they are not productive, the subject may have become overly enthusiastic, falling prey to "false memories" and similar constructions of a gullible ego.

Reincarnation Cards embodies an imaginative and novel technique, for which patents are pending, that was specifically designed to probe into one's hypothetical reincarnations. Its model of the ubiquity of mind and the simultaneity of events provides a provocative perspective on the nature and origin of the fleeting images and snatches of recollections of other eras. Numerous anecdotal reports exist from people who have glimpsed, from time to time, events and activities that occurred before they were born. Whether these glimpses represent past-life memories, archetypes of the psyche, or metaphors of current life activities, they can be linked with and evoked by the cards, following the suggested rituals described by the authors.

The evocation of these purported scenarios is not, however, the sole purpose of this project, which is intended to lead ultimately to the expansion of the consciousness of the user. Although from Ecclesiastes we learn that "there is no new thing under the sun," there are, nevertheless, new ways to present hoary old insights to new audiences or to old audiences that are newly ready to receive them. What the authors have tried to do is to present the "perennial philosophy" (the core of all spiritual traditions) in a form that will appeal to interested people who rarely have been exposed to such ideas. To this end, what the authors call for is a fresh look at consciousness, in other words the pattern of awareness, intention, and reflection that permeates the cosmos.

The authors suggest that if we can somehow learn to set aside our emotional entanglement with our belief in our separate individuality, we may come to perceive the world very differently. They suggest that we are conditioned from birth to think in a dualistic, reductionistic way. Our personal egos are massaged and nurtured to maturity by our parents, siblings, teachers, and peers, to accept without question the idea that the world is "outside" and that the mind is confined "within" our heads. As a consequence, we become locked into this dualistic belief system, or Gestalt, in a lifelong bondage from which, through reason and a reorientation of our personal mythology by a thorough grasp of metaphysics and the practice of meditation and contemplation, we are capable of liberating ourselves, thereby replacing naive belief with realized knowledge.

The authors point out that a more holistic way to look at the world is to fathom that our perceptions have been blurred by what might be called "ego-spectacles." To people involved in dualistic thinking, the world is obviously "out there." The authors' monistic position, supported by some of the greatest thinkers in the history of philosophy, is that we live and move and have our being in an ocean of consciousness. This means that everything that we perceive, including the so-called external world, as well as our bodies with their sense organs and what we regard as our individual personalities, exists wholly and entirely in and as a field of consciousness.

From this very simple but profound change of perspective, it may be seen that there actually is no external world in the sense in which most people naively assume there is one. As a result, our common understanding of the world is effectively turned inside out. This involves a transformation to a new paradigm wherein one perceives and experiences the same world, but in a novel and different way. While the world is still external to the body, that same world is now understood to be internal to the mind. The "individual person," or "ego-self," is now recognized to be one with what can be called the "All-Self." In what can be described as a discerning state of "flow," there is an awareness of both the ego-self and the All-Self, in which one may identify with the latter without losing contact with the former. This "flow" precludes a disruption in the mainstream of ordinary, ongoing, day-to-day activities. In this light, the other person is no longer a stranger but oneself. Aggressive wars are unthinkable, as we should then be harming only ourselves. This, in sum, is the metaphysics on which the authors have based this project.

The authors have written an intriguing chapter titled *Human Origins*. While I remain skeptical regarding many details of their account of human prehistory or what they refer to as protohistory, I do not know of anything directly contrary to what they state in this book about humanity's obscure origins. Indeed, I am impressed by their extensive bibliography. The purpose of this controversial chapter, which is intended to be read prior to using the cards, is to open new areas for serious investigation, stimulating the imagination of those who come into contact with the cards.

I have known John and Linda for a number of years. I have met them at conferences and have visited them in their home in

Cyprus. I can vouch for their personal integrity and the purity of their motives. They have clearly labored long and hard to place this work before a public that they believe to be ready for the expansion of consciousness that is urgently needed today. Our world is driven by ignorant, egomaniacal leaders, who by waging endless wars, threaten to bring the human experiment to an ugly, ignominious end. Our civilization may be totally destroyed — not by natural cataclysms, but by our own false beliefs and dysfunctional personal myths that induce us to slaughter each other for what we erroneously believe to be our personal or tribal gain.

The injunction by an Egyptian Ger-Maa, or sage, Amen-em-Apt, at the close of the commentary on the Egypt card (No. 18) to: *Seat thyself in the arms of God. Fill thyself full of silence. Thou shalt find the Life . . .* encapsulates the entire message of this stunning, consciousness-expanding work.

❈ ❈ ❈

Stanley Krippner, Ph.D., Professor of Psychology at Saybrook Graduate School in San Francisco, is known internationally for his pioneering work in the scientific investigation of human consciousness. He has authored or edited over five hundred articles and books and conducts research in the areas of dreams, hypnosis, shamanism and dissociation, with an emphasis on anomalous phenomena that seem to question mainstream paradigms.

"I went in search of myself."

Herákleitos, 6th century BCE

⌘ ⌘ ⌘

"The journey of a thousand miles begins with a single step."

"On hearing of the Way, the best of men will earnestly explore its length. The mediocre person learns of it and takes it up and sets it down. But vulgar people will laugh out loud, and if they did not laugh, it would not be the Way."

Lao Tze, 6th century BCE

Preface

For nearly twenty years, we have lived in storied Paphos on the Eastern Mediterranean island of Cyprus, set like a jewel in the wine-dark sea of Homeric legend. From our veranda, we watch the sun set over a sea unobstructed all the way to Crete, a little over three hundred miles away to the west. Our home is the same distance north of the pyramids of Egypt, some 450 miles southeast of fabled Troy and 250 miles northwest of Jerusalem. We are only a few miles from where the goddess Aphrodite (Venus) is said to have arrived in Cyprus, wafted to Paphos as related by Homer in the Odyssey. For at least a dozen centuries before the advent of Christianity, her Temple Sanctuary attracted pilgrims from all over the Mediterranean world.

Just across the bay from our home is the peninsula where the Achaean Greeks first landed in 1250 BCE. Now an archaeological preserve, it was more recently occupied by a Roman garrison during the governorship of the Proconsul, Cicero. The whole island of Cyprus was once gifted by Antony to Cleopatra, more than a thousand years before it was taken by the Crusader King Richard the Lionhearted. Subsequently, the Knights Templar, the medieval Venetians, the Ottoman Turks and the Imperial British ruled in turn and left their traces here. Sadly, the strife and conflict continue to the present day. The island of Cyprus, the very first Christian country, is still divided by ethnic discord, a legacy of conquering armies, both current and past.

In such an historic crossroads of civilizations and cultures, with ancient sacred sites in abundance virtually on our doorstep, there is no doubt that the psychic imprints of our environs have influenced us. It is hardly surprising that we should have developed a special interest in, among other things, the much misunderstood doctrine of reincarnation.

This work has been some years in the making. It was inspired, at least in part, by the realization that the average person has only a vague and somewhat romantic idea of the subject. Reincarnation is widely interpreted as the wandering of an individual human soul through a series of physical embodiments, in the course of which it encounters the same soul-mate(s) and friends, over and over again, in repeated loving, and occasionally tragic relationships. While on one level there may be some truth in this view, we believe that it is not the whole story and that the time has come to establish reincarnation theory on a philosophically sound basis. Throughout this book the appeal is to the reason that leads to genuine knowledge, rather than to mere belief. Accordingly we suggest that, at least for the time that you are pursuing these studies, you lay aside all preconceived ideas.

This work is a "far memory recovery" technique, an apparatus for personal awareness training for which patents are currently pending. More than this, however, *Reincarnation Cards* and the accompanying book are, in effect, a course in the higher philosophy that is not essentially different from Gnosticism in the West or from philosophic (aspárśa) yoga, Taoism and Zen in the East, but stripped of all such labels. We have provided a *Glossary* to explain the precise meaning of such philosophic concepts as used throughout this book, which may differ from the conventional dictionary definitions.

In the *Republic*, Plato (427–347 BCE) declared that "Pure knowledge is the knowledge of that which always is, and not of something which at some time comes into being and then passes away." Plato thus defined the Logos, the timeless, spaceless *That* which is ultimately *real*. Contained within the Logos are all ephemeral phenomena, transient things that "pass away," including what we normally think of as our individual selves. We normally believe, mistakenly, that we are eternally separate and apart both from each other and from the Logos, reality itself.

Plato's teaching is the essence of Gnosticism as it is of the Vedanta and of other higher philosophies, both Eastern and Western. This book is based on the metaphysical doctrine that only one being, the Logos, or Cosmic Mind is real; that all phenomena, including ourselves, exist as temporary projections within that Mind; that the universe is a display of mind, by mind, to mind. This mentalist metaphysics carefully discriminates between *reality* and *existence*, declaring that mind is the *only* reality — the changeless *That* which *always is*. The existent comprises changeable phenomena that are manifested and animated by Mind. Hence the universe may certainly be said to *exist*, but it derives its *apparent* reality from that of the Cosmic Mind that generates it.

The perishable individual egoic mind is comparable to a wave on the ocean's surface. Looking out at other waves, coming into momentary existence, only virtually instantaneously to disappear and be replaced by others, the individual wave may perceive itself as unique, wholly separate from and independent of all other waves, and even mourn the appearance of birth and death amongst its companions and as its own fate. Yet all such illusions are dispelled once it looks *within* and realizes its boundless, immortal, essential nature, its true self, as *ocean*.

If faithfully followed, the successful completion of your self-directed research will provide you with an impregnable, realized knowledge, both of yourself and of the world that you appear intermittently to inhabit. This *gnosis* will be firmly based on a solid metaphysics, illumined by the practical mystical experience that will inevitably be induced by the very nature of your studies.

It now remains only to invite you to share what we offer to you in this work. If at first you fail to progress, we urge you to keep on trying. Allow this knowledge to soak completely into your understanding. The dawn may come at any time.

John Knowles and Linda Leblanc
Paphos, Cyprus

One . . . INTRODUCTION

Reincarnation is a phenomenon that fascinates everyone. What is it that incarnates? What is the soul? Do we have the same personality from life to life? The same sex, or indeed, alternatively, any sex at all? Answers to these questions, and more, are now about to become accessible to you.

There can no longer be any doubt that through projected temporary personalities you, the higher individuality, have vicariously experienced countless lives in a multitude of environments and cultures. There is now overwhelming evidence of the truth of reincarnation. This has been not only scientifically established by eminent scientific researchers, but also confirmed by an enormous and growing body of anecdotal evidence provided by numerous psychiatrists, clinical psychologists and past-life therapists. Such professionals, employing hypnosis, have evoked memories of what appear to be past and future lives from many thousands of patients. Although some reservations have been expressed about the validity of past-life regression under hypnosis, there are countless reputable therapists who obtain such information under the most stringent conditions. Reincarnation must now be regarded as a *fact*, not a fantasy. No reasonable person who examines the evidence with an open mind can fail to be convinced of its truth.

What is not generally understood, however, is the actual mechanism involved. This lack of an identifiable mechanical, cause-and-effect explanation, has resulted in the reluctance of the mainstream scientific Establishment as a whole, i.e., other than exceptional, but increasingly more numerous, individual researchers, to take anything but a skeptical position on the matter. Materialist-reductionist scientists recognize only physical matter as real or important, an assumption dating from Newton and Descartes that has hampered modern scientific thought since the seventeenth century. They reject all spiritual or other values that cannot be reduced to fit into their narrow view of reality. Nevertheless, quite aside from the evidence adduced by leading-edge scientific investigators, a growing number of psychiatrists who employ hypnosis or guided imagery as a method to uncover hidden phobias and other subconscious elements of the psyche, as well as many hypnotherapists, have found, often to their initial surprise, that they have inadvertently evoked memories of previous incarnations from their clients during the course of analysis or treatment. Many psychiatrists, like Dr. Brian Weiss, have gone on to study the phenomenon in depth and have published a number of books on the subject. Another famous psychiatrist, Dr. Ian Stevenson has reported, *inter alia,* that many children carry memories of an earlier incarnation with them. Such memories in children are normally repressed, at least in Western societies, to the point that they are quickly forgotten. There are, nevertheless, rare individuals, such as the late Michael Talbot, who have carried over more or less complete memories of earlier apparent incarnations that they have managed to retain into adulthood.

You should know that at the deepest level of what psychology calls your unconscious mind, *you already possess* full and detailed knowledge, not only of every past incarnation you have ever known through an emanated personality, but also of every incarnation you will ever vicariously experience in "time."

This book provides you with full instructions on how the associated *Reincarnation Cards* are to be most effectively utilized to recover this lost knowledge. You are also provided with a comprehensive list of recommended books and other resources on the subject for deeper study. Further research is highly recommended; it will help to familiarize you more and more with the subject of reincarnation. This will make it ever easier for you to revive your own far memory of the circumstances of other apparent embodiments.

Reincarnation Cards is not a card game, nor is it intended to be used in any form of "reading" or fortune-telling. Used properly, it is a psychological research tool that is intended to be taken seriously by the lay user. Its primary purpose is to enable you, as a person who is interested in the reincarnation phenomenon, to evoke incidents from other apparent embodiments, so-called far memories, in the form of intuitions from your own higher consciousness. Using the cards in this way, you alone are involved as the sole participant in this self-directed research. You may, of course, choose to use these cards in collaboration with a professional such as a psychiatrist, a clinical psychologist, a past-life therapist, or even with an interested friend. As already noted, many professionals have learned, through experience with their clients, that reincarnation must now increasingly be considered as factual.

What is unique about *Reincarnation Cards* is that they are designed to awaken your own intuition, to allow your conscious, egoic mind, in present-day "reality," to obtain access to knowledge of other vicariously experienced incarnations — knowledge that is already full and complete in the deeper and higher levels of consciousness. If faithfully and persistently followed, this process will stimulate the emergence into your conscious awareness of the far memory of events that were once directly known and experienced but have since been simply forgotten. This forgetfulness is believed to be caused by the overwhelming, screening influence of the gestation period, the birth trauma, early environmental circumstances including parental suppression, subsequent peer pressure, and conventional education (with its emphasis on a now out-dated reductionist, dualistic materialism and its arbitrary exclusion of anything that does not fall within the range of its own very limited laboratory methods and physical instruments).

Used as directed, the cards and their associated material as described in this book make it possible for you fairly comprehensively to reconstitute the basic characteristics of entire past, and indeed future, vicariously experienced lifetimes.

Two . . . THE EVIDENCE

he most recent pioneering scientific research clearly indicates that the reincarnation experience is a fact. The impeccable, scholarly, worldwide research of Dr. Ian Stevenson, former Carlson Professor of Psychiatry at the University of Virginia Medical School, conducted in accord with the strictest scientific protocol, has demonstrated beyond all reasonable doubt that reincarnated individuals can, and often do, carry over into the new incarnation *actual physical evidence* of traumas suffered in or other signs related to immediately preceding embodiments. (Stevenson 1997). This solid physical evidence convincingly rebuts the objections raised by skeptics, who heretofore have usually dismissed valid memories of other incarnations as mere "anecdote," hence unworthy of serious consideration.

The basic principle in physics is that all existence (i.e., the universe) is by definition, one. Monism, be it material or mental, is logically unassailable. Research into the nature of matter over the past century, however, strongly reinforces the *mental* monist view that consciousness is all; that "matter," as such, is illusory. Physicist J.S. Bell's determination of non-locality in a superluminal universe, which implies universal simultaneity (i.e., everything is really happening at once), supports this position. Accepting the 1918 Nobel Prize for Physics, the father of quantum physics, Max Planck, declared, "*There is no matter as such!* All matter originates and exists only by virtue of a force . . . We must assume behind this force the existence of a conscious and intelligent mind. This mind is the matrix of all matter."

Other outstanding scientists have had similar insights into the true nature of Reality:

Erwin Schrödinger (Nobel Physics Prize 1933):
> "Consciousness is that by which the world first becomes manifest, by which . . . it first becomes present: that the world *consists of* the elements of consciousness . . . their multiplicity [of minds] is only apparent, in truth there is only one mind. . . . Mind is always *now*. There is really no before or after for mind . . . Mind has erected the objective outside world . . . out of its own stuff." (Schrödinger 1958)

Louis de Broglie (Nobel Physics Prize 1939):
> "In space-time, everything which for each of us constitutes the past, the present and the future is given *en bloc* . . . each observer, as his or her time passes, discovers, so to speak, new slices of space-time which appear to him or her as successive aspects of the material world, though in reality the ensemble of events constituting space-time *exists prior to his or her knowledge of it*." (de Broglie 1959)

Albert Einstein (Nobel Physics Prize 1921):

"For us convinced physicists, the distinction between past, present and future is only a stubbornly persistent illusion . . . time is not at all what it seems. It does not flow in only one direction, and *the future exists simultaneously with the past.*" (Einstein 1955)

Sir James Jeans:

"The universe begins to look more like a great thought than like a great machine . . . The old dualism of mind and matter seems likely to disappear . . . through substantial matter resolving itself into a creation and manifestation of mind." (Jeans 1930)

"This brings us very near to those philosophical systems which regard the universe as a thought in the mind of its Creator, thereby reducing all discussion of material creation to futility." (Jeans 1931)

Sir Arthur Eddington:

"The stuff of the world is mind-stuff . . . The realistic matter and fields of force of former physical theory are altogether irrelevant — except in so far as the mind-stuff has itself spun these imaginings . . . It is difficult for a physicist to accept the view that the substratum of everything is of a mental character. But no one can deny that mind is the first and most direct thing in our experience, and all else is remote inference. . . . Recognizing that the physical world is entirely abstract and without 'actuality' apart from its linkage to consciousness, we restore consciousness to the fundamental position . . . The idea of a universal mind or Logos would be, I think, a fairly plausible inference from the present state of scientific theory." (Eddington 1930)

As Arthur Koestler has pointed out, "Since the concept of matter itself has been dematerialised by the physicists, materialism can no longer claim to be a scientific philosophy." (Koestler 1975)

It follows that belief in the *independent* reality of something called "matter" is a fallacy, based on an unproved and unprovable *assumption* that has hobbled and warped scientific thinking for centuries. Within the obvious unity and wholeness of existence, materialist thinkers, following Descartes, have gratuitously divided existence into a "material" world of "extended physical objects" and a "conceptual" world of "mental objects" (i.e., thoughts, feelings and beliefs). This separatist doctrine has been widely accepted for the past three and a half centuries, by modern, but non-quantum scientists, resulting in their adoption of a reductionist, dualist materialism, an attitude which stubbornly persists, although it has already been thoroughly undermined by the implications of their own research.

THE ILLUSION OF CHANGE

Long ago, Herákleitos observed that no one can twice enter the same river. Kratýlos noted that one cannot do this even once, as one is oneself always changing. It is a continuing wonder that humankind can be aware of change taking place all around them, yet, blinded by its familiarity, fail to grasp its meaning.

Anything that comes into existence at one moment of time must go out of existence at another moment of time. Everything is *constantly* changing. Nothing remains the same for two consecutive instants. Obviously, contrary to common opinion, *there is no fixed, "material" reality!* But what is actually happening?

In truth, every atom, every sub-atomic particle of "matter" is a fresh projection in consciousness each tiny fraction of a second. This incredibly small interval between "frames," one tenth of a trillionth of a trillionth of a second (10^{-23}s) has actually been calculated by physicists. Accordingly, "material reality" is a continual succession of extremely rapidly projected images. Just as one ignores the projector while at the cinema, accepting that the sounds and sights on the screen truly represent external reality rather than a smoothly blended succession of still images, so one is lured by its continuity into the false belief that "things" exist as solid "matter," "outside" and separate from our consciousness — "matter" that *somehow* changes in time, with no attempt being made to understand this process. Yet, on closer introspection, one may glimpse the underlying, unchanging awareness that is the silent witness to the constant flux of change. All sensations, perceptions, exist within this consciousness. How else would one even become aware of change, except in relation to the changeless? Normally we fail to realize that the entire panorama is only an enormous, complex event *in* consciousness, i.e., an idea that is projected through us, and that *includes* us. The question now arises, Who or what is the projector?

We know that consciousness and its products are *all that we ever actually experience*, and that consciousness is clearly primal and ubiquitous, a fact which is coming increasingly to be recognized by the most advanced scientists themselves. Thoroughly to understand this involves a *Gestalt Switch*, a complete transformation to a new paradigm, wherein one perceives the same world, but in an entirely new and different way. The universe is no longer "out there." It is "in here." This "new" way of perceiving the world is merely a restatement of ancient wisdom, which declares that all that any individual knows is known *only* in consciousness; that *all* is consciousness, *so far as one knows, or can ever know*. According to this mentalist view, the universe is not composed of an hypothesized matter, but is the manifestation in time and space of one infinite superconscious Being, or Cosmic Mind. This Cosmic Mind, to which the individual's conscious and unconscious egoic mind are *essentially* connected, contains all knowledge of all creatures and events, past, present and future, in a timeless NOW. In relation to you as an individual, higher-level being, it contains, *inter alia*, your complete incarnational history, past and future.

REFERENCES

de Broglie, Louis (1959), "A General Survey of the Scientific Work of Albert Einstein." In Schillp, Paul Arthur (Ed). *Albert Einstein Philosopher–Scientist*, NY, Evanston & London, Harper & Row, Harper Torchbook edition.

Eddington, Sir Arthur (1930), *The Nature of the Physical World*, NY Macmillan/Cambridge University Press.

Einstein, Albert (1955), "Correspondence with Michelangelo Besso 1903–1955." P. Speziali (Ed) Hermann, Paris 1972. Quoted in Coveney, Peter & Roger Highfield. *The Arrow of Time*, London, Flamingo 1991.

Jeans, Sir James (1931), *The Universe Around Us*, NY, Macmillan/Cambridge University Press.

Jeans, Sir James (1930), *The Mysterious Universe,* NY, Macmillan/Cambridge University Press.

Koestler, Arthur (1975), "Order from Disorder". In Hardy, Alister, Robert Harvie & Arthur Koestler, *The Challenge of Chance,* NY, Random House/First Vintage Books Edition.

Schrödinger, Erwin (1958), *What is Life?*, Cambridge University Press.

Stevenson, Ian (1966), *Twenty Cases Suggestive of Reincarnation*, Charlottesville, U of Virginia Press.

Stevenson, Ian (1987), *Children who Remember Past Lives*, Charlottesville, U of Virginia Press.

Stevenson, Ian (1997), *Where Reincarnation and Biology Intersect*, Westport, Ct., Praeger. *

---

* This most important, 200-page work condenses a much longer one entitled *Reincarnation and Biology: A Contribution to the Etiology of Birthmarks and Birth Defects*, a medical monograph with extensive documentation, references, numerous tables and many footnotes. It is discussed further in No. A-19 of the Bibliography.

It is strongly recommended that you acquire this and all of Dr. Stevenson's published works to form the basis for your own research library.

Three . . . BENEFITS

Your acquaintance with past and future incarnations leads to absolute fearlessness. No longer a matter of mere belief, you will know that the real you can never die; that you are birthless as well as deathless. Your various bodily forms, projected personalities and apparently outer circumstances come and go in time, but consciousness is forever. You *are*. Death is now seen simply to be only a transition from one temporary, limited state of consciousness to another. Hence the first great benefit of full realization of the fact of reincarnation is that it removes entirely the fear of death that is normally experienced by virtually all people at some time and by some people all of the time.

There are other benefits as well. Many mental, emotional and physical tendencies are brought over by the higher individuality and incorporated into the current personality, the secondary individual that you normally consider to be the everyday you. There are many common physical conditions that may and often do have relevance to a previous incarnation, such as chronic headaches and other pains, back and neck problems and allergies. Mental and emotional problems such as severe depression, suicidal tendencies, Multiple Personality Disorder, Dissociative Identity Disorder and schizophrenia have also been found, upon investigation, frequently to be past-life related. Most of these, to some extent, may yield to past-life therapy, often to complete remission.

There are certain particular indications of past lives to watch for. These include: a compulsion to overeat; a craving for or repulsions toward particular foods; and apparently irrational fears (phobias) of snakes, fire, water, flying, crowds, earthquakes and other natural cataclysms, travel, open spaces, closed spaces, heights, the dark, and certain colors such as red, "creepy crawlies," etc. Most phobias of unknown etiology may be and often are eliminated by past-life therapy.

It has been said that there is scarcely a single aspect of character or human behavior that cannot be better understood through an examination of past-life events. Just as phobias caused by traumatic experiences in early childhood can often be overcome when their source is identified, so certain phobias and even physical handicaps that have their source as a sort of psychic inheritance from earlier incarnations, can also be eliminated. These tend to disappear once they are consciously encountered and recognized.

CAUTION

Be warned once again, however, that *Reincarnation Cards Awakening Far Memory* is not a game. It is a serious research tool, the ultimate purpose of which is to accelerate your spiritual growth through the greater knowledge and insight to be derived from having ever more free access to your personal history through the incarnations.

The glimpses that you obtain into your previous or indeed future projected personalities may not always be pleasant. Like your life today, your other apparent life experiences are a mixed bag of joys and sorrows, gains and losses, likes and dislikes, loves and hates, births and deaths. Some of what you learn may at first be somewhat painful. It is not for nothing that a merciful Nature has drawn a veil across past and future that prevents you from normally having direct, unimpeded access to the complete memory of earlier, or indeed future, lives.

Nevertheless, you will find that these materials have placed in your hands the master key to unlock the gate that leads to an understanding of the ultimate mysteries of life and death.

As your knowledge of your past and future lives grows, the cumulative effect will lead to your realization of the transient nature of the human condition. You will uncover various lives that have been vicariously experienced by your many different projected personalities. As you view them, it will slowly dawn on you just how fleeting is the experience of life in the physical body. Since you will see that every apparent embodiment involved a somewhat different personality, as you note one such ephemeral mask, or persona, succeeded by another, sometimes differing greatly, you will view the passage of your many lives with a growing sense of detachment. You will become increasingly aware of the serene, impersonal observer, the timeless, higher individuality, *Overself*, or Atman, that has *apparently* projected these various personalities into incarnation.

This higher individuality, itself timeless and changeless, appears to send out different personalities to release and to develop their own potentialities, while remaining, itself unmoved, forever still at the center. This whole Self may be compared to a wheel. Utterly still at the center, each of its myriad spokes is a separate incarnation, every one outwardly different from but intimately linked to every other one. The higher individuality looks upon each of its incarnate emanations impersonally. Moreover, it does not view them sequentially. It grasps the entire universe and everything in it, past, present and future, in one vast vision, in one all-timed fixity. Hence the cards have a higher purpose: to awaken your intuition to the full, leading you to the supreme, all-embracing insight into That which is ultimately *real*, behind all such phenomena. You will then know that, as consciousness itself, you are *essentially* identical to the Logos, Cosmic Mind, and that as such, you are therefore incarnate in all things, in all times and in all places *simultaneously*. You will then clearly see that all births, deaths, personalities and incarnations are ephemeral phenomena of no *ultimate* significance other than to guide you to *discover for yourself* this final, complete understanding both of your higher Self and of your identity with the Universal or Cosmic Mind.

Four . . . HUMAN ORIGINS

^{(*}**A**^{*)}s your primary interest in this research is to gain direct access to details of your prior and future human and other apparent embodiments, it may be helpful to understand the human historical framework within which your research will be conducted. What will be disclosed here is the essential truth, so far as is known, of human physical history, although it may well be subject to adjustment in minor details. As your studies progress, you will be able, more and more, to fill in the blanks for yourself. Although there is some evidence to support the hypothesis, the question of the possible partial extra-terrestrial origin of humankind will not be explored here.

Much of what follows will likely be found to be at least questionable by conventional scientists, who are locked into their own limited materialist, reductionist belief systems. Nevertheless, this information is essentially true, as you shall certainly find out for yourself if you follow faithfully the guidelines provided in this book. The technique of self-awareness embedded in these *Reincarnation Cards* relies on the stimulation of subtle, intuitive knowings. We have therefore deliberately not included extensive footnotes and references to much of what follows, as such interruptions could well interfere with the spontaneous flow of perceptions.

The extensive Bibliography at the end of this book lists many references that provide evidence of the mysterious origins and history of humankind and of the cyclical destruction of ancient civilizations on this planet. If the reader is unfamiliar with this extensive research, we encourage the undertaking of an in-depth study of this fascinating field of enquiry. Many meticulous and ethical researchers, digging beyond Establishment assumptions, have devoted their lives to achieving a better understanding of our history. The writings of these pioneers are a precious resource for the open-minded researcher who seeks the truth. The time and effort spent in studying these alternative views of history will embark the reader on an intellectually stimulating and challenging voyage through the ages that will greatly expand the areas open to psychic exploration.

A common theme in the *Reincarnation Cards* is the natural series of sudden, intermittent, catastrophic destructions of civilizations. This emphasis is deliberate. Recovery of far memory is frequently associated with the impact on conscious awareness of extremely traumatic events. In addition, with a deepening understanding of the length and breadth of human history, there comes a growing insight into the greater cyclical process of apparent incarnation. The rise and fall of species, of cultures, and indeed of individuals — all of these are seen with ever greater clarity to be but aspects of the whole — a microcosm within the Cosmic Mind.

Little is known with certainty about the very early years of our species or whence it came. A great deal of what passes for science in archaeology and anthropology is little more than assumption and guesswork, based on very fragmentary evidence. What *is* known is that many times in the past this planet has been subjected to major catastrophic events, such as the impact or close passage of a Near Earth Object (NEO) like an asteroid, a large comet, or even a minor planet, that all but destroyed such life as had evolved on it up to that time. According to the geological record, this has happened on at least five occasions in the past 440 million years, each of them marking the end of a geological era. On every such occasion, up to ninety percent of then-existent species were simply annihilated. The last of these great extinctions was that of the dinosaurs, believed to have been destroyed by an NEO strike that brought the Mesozoic Era to an end some sixty-five million years ago.

On a somewhat smaller scale, cataclysmic events that involved widespread devastation have been dated to about 7500 BCE, 6000 BCE and even as recently as 1200 BCE.

All over the world, in the traditions of literally hundreds of different cultures, there are legends that are obviously versions of the same tragic story. These are tales of utterly overwhelming catastrophes by fire or, especially, by water. They tell of cataclysmic events that, not only once but many times, have destroyed the greater part of humanity, thereby ending a Golden Age of high civilization. We learn of a vast destruction caused by great floods, such as those recorded in the Bible, the Epic of Gilgamesh and the Greek story of Deucalion, among countless others.

Devastating as all of these undoubtedly were, for sheer worldwide destructiveness they do not compare with what Solon's Egyptian priest interlocutor, who evidently knew of the intervening earlier floods, described as the "Great Deluge of All," that suddenly and catastrophically ended the Pleistocene Epoch and all but annihilated the human species in about 9600 BCE. The unspeakable horror of that dreadful time, when the Earth nearly died, is seared indelibly into the collective memory of humankind.

The Greenland glacier ice cores identify 9645 BCE as the likely actual year, consistent with Plato's account of the destruction of Atlantis. This "Great Deluge of All" may also be recorded in the legends of the extremely ancient floods of Manu in the East and of Ogyges in the West.

As the Egyptian priest also told Solon, as recorded by Plato in the *Timaeus*, events of this kind leave only an unlettered remnant of shepherds and herdsmen in the higher hills. In due course, these traumatized survivors cautiously descend from the mountains to the clean-swept lowlands to begin, once again, the long climb to civilization.

The memory banks of humankind were, not for the first or even the last time, all but wiped clean. A worldwide high, maritime civilization capable of mapping, and that demonstrably *did* map the entire globe, had been totally destroyed.

Apart from whatever other evidence may have survived, traces of this earth-shattering event are to be found today in the form of ancestral and reincarnational far memories of the long-lost ages; periods during which one may, through emanated personalities, have vicariously experienced existences in such fabled cultures as those of "Mu" and "Atlantis."

Although largely dismissed as unlikely by conventional archaeology, physical evidence of such a protohistory has been steadily emerging here and there. This evidence is strong enough to challenge the current conservative belief system of the archae-ological Establishment.

Ignorant of the remote past, and deliberately restricting themselves to the study of early, post-diluvial cultures and the rarely found physical, skeletal remains of early humans and apes, primarily in Africa and in Western Europe, modern anthropolo-gists have laboriously constructed a plausible, if superficial and very incomplete, picture of the physical evolution of modern *homo sapiens*. This is stated to have begun only a couple of hundred thousand years ago, derived from an apelike progenitor who first emerged in Africa perhaps five to ten million years earlier. From there, humankind are said to have spread to the other continents. The latest of these migrations was allegedly to the Americas from Asia, via Beringia, no earlier than about

10,000 BCE, although recent discoveries in the Americas have now pushed this date back by many millennia. There is evidence of recognizably modern human habitation of the Americas for at least the past three hundred thousand years.

Moreover, the human body itself provides evidence, in the form of relative hairlessness, bipedalism, a subcutaneous fat layer, webbed digits, the descended larynx and the ability to shed tears, that evolved in humans alone of the primates. This suggests a physical evolutionary period of at least one to two million years in an aquatic environment in very ancient times. Typically, conventional scientists simply ignore this evidence, openly visible to everyone by physical inspection, simply because it does not fit their assumptions (see Bibliography B: Morgan).

In fairness, it must be said that European and North American anthropologists were initially gravely handicapped by early exposure to the Judaeo-Christian version of the history of humanity as recorded in the Bible. A surprisingly large number of people, even including credentialed scientists, still believe that the world was literally created in 4004 BCE. This alleged year of Creation is still printed in some versions of the Bible, at the very beginning of Genesis.

In an understandable over-reaction to such inherited beliefs, most conventional anthropologists, now commendably cautious, have carefully restricted themselves to selected physical evidence in the form of the skeletal remains and the tools of so-called primitive humans. Yet it has been said that all of the skeletal remains that have been thus accepted could be stored in a box measuring only a couple of cubic meters. There is really very little here on which to construct an elaborate theory of human physical evolution. Moreover, in the naïve belief that they know more about the history of the various peoples than the people themselves, materialist scientists reject, as mere fanciful myth, all indigenous historical accounts that conflict with their own timetable. In its determination not to be influenced by biblical-type stories, anthropology has been unwilling to accept or even to examine seriously the anecdotal testimony of virtually every ancient human group, ignoring the traditions of literally hundreds of different cultures.

The conventional, so called "scientific" view, based on a reductionist materialism and an increasingly questionable neo-Darwinist, purely mechanical version of a gradual human physical evolution in a non-catastrophic environment, has hardened into a cast-iron dogma. We are expected to accept without question the belief that the earliest modern human beings emerged, at most, only a couple of hundred thousand years ago in Africa and that our most recent, direct ancestors, the Cro-Magnons, suddenly appeared in Europe only about thirty-five thousand to forty thousand years ago. In this view, humankind evolved to their present eminence in an incredibly short space of time through an altogether unlikely series of accidental coincidences, ascribed to a process of natural selection leading to the survival of the fittest. In this context, it has been said that the creation of the higher forms of life purely by chance is similar to the chance that a tornado sweeping through a junkyard might assemble a Boeing 747. In fact, it is now known to be quite impossible for physical evolution to have occurred at all without, in some manner, the genetic transmission of acquired characteristics to future generations. The most recent cellular research into epigenetics has actually discovered the mechanism of this transmission, thus, to some extent, restoring to respectability the formerly much-maligned evolutionary theories of Lamarck, Michurin and Lysenko (see Bibliography B: Lipton).

It is not so much that Darwinism is necessarily wrong but that without regard to consciousness, it is woefully incomplete. The materialist sees the world as separate and distinct from its inhabitants, who are all, in turn, forever separate and distinct from each other. "Things" may be "objectively" studied without reference to the observer. Consciousness is declared to be an epiphenomenon; that is, a chemical secretion of, and limited to, the brain. This materialist-reductionist view signally fails to perceive the underlying unity of a shared existence in a universal consciousness. Materialists reject the vital principle, Cosmic Mind, the very self and soul of the universe, the intuitive apprehension of which by humans has given rise to all religions. Considering religion as nothing but superstition, materialists ignore their own spiritual Source and recognize only mechanical forces of nature as having any relevance to their research.

Consequently, they reject all of the obvious indications of intelligent design in the world's creatures, both individually and, especially, in how they relate to each other in an all but incredible interwoven complexity, the whole united in a vast cosmic harmony. They consider advocacy of a unifying cosmic intelligence to be merely an effort to introduce an unacceptable Creationism via the back door. Materialists who see only blind, mechanical forces physically acting on each other, with no underlying unity in consciousness, are to be pitied for their own blindness.

In the course of time, the progressively hardening position of conventional science has led to the rejection of any evidence, however soundly-based, that cannot be made to fit into the rigid, materialist framework of the world's history that has been decreed by the Establishment as the only acceptable one. Intellectual positions have been solidified. University chairs are now occupied by a virtual priesthood of *Scientism*, the new orthodox religion. These academics regard any new, contradictory evidence of extremely ancient human culture as a personal threat. To experts whose continued financial prosperity and professional status depend on the maintenance of the *status quo*, the idea that textbooks might have to be rewritten and that they themselves might, in effect, have to return to the classroom, is totally unacceptable. Their vested interests must be protected at all costs.

Truth is always the first casualty in such a situation. The scientistic Establishment has erected a pseudo-scientific screen, through which evidence can be admitted only if it supports the authorized version of history. Everything that does not fit in is simply ignored. Any Establishment "priest" who privately deviates from the received dogma must remain silent or expect to be pilloried as a heretic, to be persecuted and expelled from the priesthood. Many honest and courageous dissident scientists have already been subjected to this shabby treatment.

There is, however, a great and growing body of evidence of the presence of anatomically modern human beings having lived on this planet not merely thousands, not hundreds of thousands, but even many millions of years ago (see Bibliography B: Cremo and Thompson, Corliss). The evidence, if it were to be allowed, is very persuasive, but it simply cannot even gain admission into the academic discussion. Nevertheless, there are times when the scientistic Establishment, try as it may, cannot prevent the introduction of evidence that completely upsets the conventional view of history. This happens when a relatively soft social science, such as archaeology, is directly confronted by a hard, physical science like geology.

One glaring example of this collision is the continued willful and deliberate failure of the conventional Egyptological hierarchy to deal with the earth-shaking implications of the stubborn geological fact that the Egyptian Sphinx and the walls of the Sphinx Enclosure show unmistakable evidence of weathering by exposure to long centuries, indeed millennia, of heavy rainfall rather than of erosion by wind-driven sand (see Bibliography B: West). This assessment, supported by virtually all geologists other than a mere handful who have been carefully selected and coached by the Establishment to reflect its own prejudice, proves that the Sphinx *must* be much older, by many thousands of years, than the age (2500 BCE) conventionally assigned to it by academic Egyptology. Yet, just as the inquisitors refused to look through Galileo's telescope, today's Egyptologists stubbornly refuse to take an unbiased look at the evidence.

Awkwardly, given the renown of the Sphinx and its popularity as a tourist attraction for thousands of educated, open-minded visitors every year, this evidence is of a sort that *cannot* be filtered out, as so much equally valid evidence has been successfully ignored by Establishment science in the past. Egyptologists try to pretend it does not exist, but they cannot succeed. The evidence is there, out in the open, for all to see and to judge for themselves.

Ancient sea maps afford us yet another example of scientism's obstinate refusal to face an unpalatable truth. The Haji Ahmed (1559) map accurately depicts the entire continents of North and South America with an added one thousand-mile-wide land bridge connecting America to Asia across Beringia, as it is only now known to have existed at the very height of the last (Wisconsin) Ice Age, about fifteen thousand years BCE. It should also be noted that although the Antarctic continent was allegedly first discovered by Europeans in the year 1818, the Piri Reis (1513) and Oronteus Finaeus (1531) maps clearly delineate sections of the coastline of Antarctica in detail, correctly locating rivers and bays now under the ice for at least the past six thousand years. Even more surprisingly, the Philippe Buache (1737) map essentially depicts Antarctica as it actually is *under the ice*, in a configuration unknown to moderns until the International Geophysical Year 1958, when it was clearly revealed by seismic soundings. The Buache map takes us back a million or more years to a time when Antarctica was completely ice-free (see Bibliography B: Hapgood).

These maps clearly bespeak an antiquity that exceeds, by many times over, the antiquity of the most ancient written records hitherto known to us. They have been in the public domain for centuries, but have been studiously ignored. Based on more ancient maps, now lost, they require a high, protohistoric, worldwide, maritime civilization to have produced them at all. They call for not only a knowledge of the geography itself and of spherical trigonometry but also a means of accurately determining longitude. The West did not achieve this before the late eighteenth century CE.

All of these facts, as well as unimpeachable stratigraphic evidence of the presence of anatomically modern humans on this earth *many millions* of years ago, but in the "wrong place," are greeted with a thunderous silence on the part of Establishment scientists, who hope that ignoring them will make them go away. But they *won't* go away. Sooner or later, the priesthood of scientism will be forced to examine them without bias and reluctantly to accept them in the same ungenerous spirit as the Inquisition displayed when, in 1991, it finally "rehabilitated" Galileo after a mere three and one-half centuries of dilatory circumspection.

Humankind have forgotten both their illustrious physical forebears and their divine spiritual origin. It is the purpose of the accompanying cards to enable them to remember not only what they once apparently were, but also who they now and forever are.

"Men who love wisdom must be good inquirers into many things. Nature loves to hide."

Herákleitos, 6th century BCE

Five . . . HOW TO USE THE CARDS

The Reincarnation Cards consist of five categories: Occupation, Culture, Environment, Theme and Termination. In only sixty-one cards, it is obviously impossible to cover every conceivable aspect of even one of the categories. But thousands, or even hundreds, of cards are not needed to enable you to trigger latent memories of other embodiment experiences that you have apparently undergone through the agency of your various projected personalities.

It is not the number of cards or the breadth of their coverage that is nearly so important to your success as your own attitude to this research. If you are a convinced materialist who believes that the subject of reincarnation is absolute nonsense, you will clearly have only yourself to blame if you fail to achieve positive results. If, on the contrary, you are convinced of its truth, your research will surely be far more productive and your goals reached much sooner.

One of the best ways in which to ensure early success in your research is to supplement your practice with the cards by extensive reading on the subject. This immersion in the topic will help to remove all lingering doubts as to the validity of Reincarnation Theory.

As a guide to your studies, an extensive, selected Bibliography will be found at the end of this book.

The increased knowledge will contribute in a major way not only to your success with the cards but also to your general metaphysical and spiritual understanding.

The contemplation of new ideas, however outlandish they may at first appear, can be of immense help in opening the door to ever-greater spiritual development. In a departure from the normal treatment of the subject of reincarnation, you may wish to consider the possibility, even the likelihood, that you have vicariously experienced (and indeed continue, at this very moment, to experience!) incarnations in a virtually infinite number of forms other than the human form in which you appear to be experiencing it today.

In the higher philosophical sense, it may be said that you, the real you, are actually, right now, incarnate in all things at all times and in all places. This concept, and its consequences, are further elucidated in Chapter Seven hereunder, *The Secret.*

It need not be assumed that any one card, in isolation, is particularly significant. One card should be considered in the context of other cards. Cards that are drawn together do not necessarily go together. Nevertheless, any "hand" of five cards, one from each category (Occupation, Culture, Environment, Theme, Termination) can, and often does, convey a unified picture of the circumstances of an entire incarnation.

There are 235,620 possible combinations of these five cards.

Prior to using the cards, it is recommended that you equip yourself with a pendulum (discussed below) and a loose-leaf notebook to serve as your journal.

It is recommended that the cards be used as follows:

1. Relax completely. *Take a few slow, deep breaths.* Listen to the silence to clear the mind. State your intention: that you wish to receive details of an incarnation, a knowledge of which would be helpful to you in your present life.

2. Thoroughly shuffle the cards and lay them out, on a table, in the shape of a fan or fans, facedown.

3. Ask your higher consciousness for guidance.

4. Open your mind. Think of yourself as pure consciousness. Try to eliminate all extraneous thoughts, expectations, memories. Be receptive. Simply remain open to what the cards wish to tell you.

5. Moving your hand back and forth over the cards, *allow your hand to select* a card from each of the five kinds. Alternatively, you may use the pendulum in one hand, lightly touching each card with the other and letting the pendulum indicate which card to choose.

6. As you turn each card over, watch for and record your first impression(s). Let its broad meaning reach out to

you. Examine it, keeping always an open, relaxed state of mind, inviting your higher consciousness to come to the fore.

7. Read the text associated with the card and pay heed to any suggestions or resonances that arise. Think about them, trying to trace such clues to their source in your far memory.

8. Make a note in your notebook of any evoked intuitions, especially first impressions.

NB: The genuine intuition is a subtle *knowing* that manifests best on its own, when you detach yourself from conscious thought. Flashes of intuition will come, but no particular intuition necessarily means too much by itself. Hence the importance of the notebook. As these impressions are recorded and subsequently collated and grouped *in the manner that suggests itself* (and it is important that you simply allow this to happen) you will gradually build up more or less coherent pictures of specific incarnations.

With increasing use, you will find that the precision with which your *higher consciousness itself* calls forth the material that is strictly relevant to your purposes is truly remarkable. Synchronicities in everyday life are experienced more and more frequently as your practice advances. As you become increasingly familiar with these intuitions, you become both more sensitive to them and more convinced of their actuality. This, in turn, stimulates the evocation of more and more of them. Because you are using a loose-leaf notebook for your journal, you will, over time, be able to reconstruct, as it were, the experiences from a variety of complete lives. When, for any one incarnation, these reach a critical mass, you may, quite suddenly, consciously recall more or less the entire history of that particular lifetime experience.

As you review each culture, each occupation, termination, etc., while quietening your normally active mind, continue to leave yourself open to the impressions, the resonances that seem to be evoked by each item. Many, if not most, will have no immediate meaning for you. Make notes of all of them anyway. Some certainly will eventually be found to be meaningful, even if not at first recognized as such. Meditate on all resonances that seem to be particularly meaningful for you. Try to remember, to trace them to their sources.

You may find yourself to be fascinated by certain periods in history and by particular geographical locations, such as Old China or India, ancient Egypt, mediaeval Italy, early Greece or Rome, the land of the Incas or the Mayas, or even World War II with its bloody battles and concentration camps. These feelings are intuitions that indicate an earlier acquaintance with those areas. The review of occupations may similarly yield a clue to activities you may have pursued in an earlier vicariously experienced life there. Again, the moon, stars and planets may engage your attention. You may be tapping into what is normally considered to be a future life. Such experiences will lead you eventually to understand that all pasts and all futures actually co-exist simultaneously, in an Eternal Now.

As indicated, all such intuitions and impressions should be carefully recorded in your journal, loose-leaf to allow for later insertions of similar intuitions, to enable them to be grouped together for analysis. They should be reviewed from time to time and added to as further intuitions emerge from the higher and deeper levels of consciousness.

You should also include, at the appropriate place in your journal, dream episodes that seem to relate to other embodiment experiences. Particular note should be taken of dreams in which you seem to adopt a *different personality* and care should be taken to record its characteristics in as great detail as you are able to recall.

All of the details of your entire incarnational history are preserved in the higher consciousness. You are prevented from normally having access to them by a barrier created by the egoic mind, the projected personality in your current incarnation. This perceived ego-personality is somewhat different in every incarnation that is projected by the birthless and deathless Higher Self, or Atman. It is conditioned by such factors, *inter alia*, as sexual orientation, genetic inheritance and various prenatal and post-natal environmental influences, all of which, in combination, contribute to what the individual in the current embodiment considers to be the personal self.

Researchers have found that one experiences apparent incarnations as both male and female, more or less equally, regardless of one's sex in the current incarnation. The ratio between the sexes of every group of projected personalities tends to be in accord with the approximately 50:50 ratio of the sexes in everyday life.

As you use the cards, the defences set up by the ego-personality of your current incarnation will, in the course of time, gradually be worn away. As early conditioning and belief systems are reviewed and evaluated at a deeper intuitive level, the process of further self-discovery provides new insights into who you really are.

Using the Pendulum

In addition to the cards themselves, the pendulum also will allow you to tap into the same higher consciousness. A pendulum is quite easy to use. It may be bought commercially or you may make your own, with nothing more complicated than a six-to-eight inch thread or string, from which you suspend a small weight, like a ring or a key.

You then train yourself in its use. Seated at a table, both feet on the floor (uncrossed ankles), rest the elbow on the table and suspend the pendulum from the hand. Try not to move it by any conscious action of your own. You then ask your higher consciousness to show you what the pendulum will do if you ask it a *Yes* or *No* question. *Yes* may be indicated by the pendulum moving in a clockwise circle, and *No* by moving counterclockwise. Alternatively, *Yes* may be by either type of circle, and *No* by a diagonal movement of the pendulum, or vice versa. With practice, you will settle on what is the correct procedure for you. Ask it only questions that can be answered by *Yes* or *No*.

There are many ways in which you can use it in your research. For example, you might try map-dowsing with a pendulum, to identify areas of the world in which you have experienced apparent lifetimes, a knowledge of which is relevant to your present incarnation. First, you might identify a particular continent on a world map, then zero in more and more accurately on larger scale maps covering smaller areas, until you may actually pinpoint a specific location of interest. The pendulum also may be used to determine the time period in which an incarnational experience apparently occurred. Perhaps the most important use of the pendulum in conjunction with the cards is to verify the accuracy of your interpretation of any given intuition.

STRUCTURE OF THE REINCARNATION CARDS SET

The cards comprise five (5) sets of *Categories*. Each set is identified by color and/or symbol. The categories and their codes are set out below:

Category	Color	Symbol		Number of Cards
Occupation	White	Square	□	14
Culture	Lapis Blue	Circle	○	17
Environment	Green	Diamond	◇	9
Theme	Red	Cross	+	11
Termination	Purple	Infinity	∞	10
Total				61

These categories are broken down into sub-categories. On the face of each card is drawn a picture indicative of some known aspect or aspects of the sub-category. For each of these cards this book provides a description and brief analysis to aid you in interpreting the significance of a particular card. The card categories and sub-categories are as follows:

☐ White Cards (14) OCCUPATION

1. Government
2. Law
3. Military
4. Health
5. Education
6. Agriculture
7. Artist ~ Artisan
8. Builder
9. Trader
10. Laborer
11. Beggar
12. Courtesan
13. Mother
14. Religious

○ Lapis Blue Cards (17) CULTURE

15. Prehistoric
16. Protohistoric
17. Mesopotamia
18. Egypt
19. Greece
20. Rome
21. Dark Ages
22. Celtic

23. Renaissance
24. Islamic
25. India ~ Southeast Asia
26. China ~ Japan
27. Central Asia ~ Tibet
28. Central America
29. South America
30. Indigenous Tribal
31. Alien

◇ Green Cards (9) ENVIRONMENT

32. Desert
33. Forest
34. Mountain
35. Fields
36. Riverine
37. Town
38. City
39. Marine
40. Seashore

+ Red Cards (11) THEME

41. Abundance ~ Penury
42. Growth
43. Justice ~ Injustice

44. Stability ~ Instability
45. Love ~ Indifference
46. Power
47. Creativity ~ Destructiveness
48. Freedom ~ Servitude
49. Greed ~ Generosity
50. Betrayal
51. Fear

∞ Purple Cards (10) TERMINATION

52. Peaceful
53. Water
54. Fire
55. War
56. Suicide
57. Attack
58. Accident
59. Disease
60. Catastrophe
61. Starvation

☐ OCCUPATION CARDS — INTRODUCTION

The fourteen cards in this category are barely adequate to cover the vast range of occupations in which one may engage. Each of them is intended to embrace an entire field of activity, in which any number of specific occupations are included.

By drawing one of these cards, it would appear that an egoic consciousness that you projected has probably been in some way associated with the indicated occupation or profession. Either you apparently practiced the profession or occupation yourself or you were in some way greatly influenced by it or by someone who did engage in it.

Indeed, at some point in your vast incarnational history you have certainly been closely acquainted on more than one occasion with all of these activities at one time or another.

Since employment normally takes up a considerable amount of one's daily activities, resonances may be felt to particular professions that left a psychic mark on you. The wide range of choices of ways to provide oneself with a livelihood may reveal many of life's challenges, ranging from the more lofty spiritual or intellectual to those of a purely materialist nature.

These Occupation cards are designed to stimulate those buried memories of careers that provided important life lessons in an apparent embodiment — resonances that may very well be reflected in your present incarnation.

1. GOVERNMENT

GOVERNMENT

Your selection of this card suggests that, through a projected personality, you have experienced an incarnation or incarnations in the course of which you played a role that involved a formal mastery over the daily lives of numbers of others, a group or groups of whom were in some sense legally subordinate to you. Whether inherited or earned, such a governing position carries with it a heavy responsibility. The temptations for abuse are correspondingly great. The manner in which you responded to the challenges that arose during that period would have been critical.

Ideally, you will have learned that a proper balance must be struck between force and magnanimity, so as to achieve a necessary respect for authority while avoiding heavy-handedness. The tyrant may be feared but is rarely loved.

Your actions during that apparent lifetime would have had a profound effect upon the lives of many others for whose welfare you were responsible. Greed is rewarded in outer appearance only. There is no lasting "material" gain. Failure to adhere to the highest ethical standards in such a situation would have had far-reaching karmic consequences that may very well have affected your current life situation.

One sign of having vicariously known an embodiment of this kind could be an innate desire to be of service to others. In some cases, this tendency could even be expressed in feelings of servility or fawning sycophancy towards those in authority. Conversely, one could have the urge to reject or actively to rebel against those in power, who are deemed to have abused their position to destroy your inalienable right to freedom as a human being.

2. LAW

Since the very beginning of civilization, human beings have found it necessary to establish rules, generally accepted by their society, to govern the activities of its individual members as they relate to each other and to their society as a whole. Long before the time of the Babylonian Hammurabi (ca. 1730–1685 BCE), such rules were authoritatively codified, officially promulgated and, in time, sanctified by tradition.

The existence of a code of laws requires that there be created a corps of police to enforce them and a system of courts in which to assess their applicability to a given situation. A class of experts in the law came into being along with it, made up of officials and judges.

The body of law and its administration have grown throughout the ages, from the very earliest protohistoric and prehistoric times, by far the greater part of which has been lost.

Your selection of this card suggests one or more projected personalities as a participant in activities revolving around legal issues. In the course of such activities you were exposed to many of the vices and foibles of the human condition throughout the ages, either as an observer or as a perpetrator of that which your society of the day deemed to be a crime.

Whatever the specifics of the circumstances may have been, you are free of any responsibility for what your projected incarnate personality may have appeared to do. Ultimately there is no sin and no divine punishment. The only punishment is a consequent failure to advance in the ability to discriminate between that which merely exists in "time" and *That* which forever *is*.

3. MILITARY

Many an embodiment has been experienced in a military situation. Your selection of this card suggests that you have projected a personality into incarnation as a soldier, or some other kind of

MILITARY

warrior, male or female, not once, but many times.

History and prehistory are full of occasions when, by either choice or necessity, you have taken up weapons to defend or to attack. Much blood has been shed both by your projected personality and by others wounded or slain by him or her. As a member of a military group of any kind, you may have experienced a sense of shared purpose of a team focused on a common goal. This requires discipline, courage and commitment, all useful life skills that may be available to you now in your current apparent embodiment.

One lesson you have surely learned is that violence and aggression are rarely the best way to achieve a purpose. Only when driven to it as a last resort should arms be taken up against others, and even then it may be considered wiser and more noble simply to "look on as the legions thunder past, then plunge in thought again."

There is no question of right or wrong in all of this. What is important for you now is to recall such bloody episodes and, by recalling them in all their shocking detail, to realize that, however vivid they may have seemed to your egoic mind at the time, they are ultimately unreal.

You and those you consider to be your enemies are, in reality, One. There is no separateness, no individuality, no "other." In the final analysis, when apparently inflicting harm on "others," you were hurting only yourself.

4. HEALTH

From the earliest times, humans have been concerned with the care and treatment of the ill and the injured. From the Neolithic shaman medicine man or woman to the modern healthcare professional, male or female, countless individuals have devoted themselves to this noblest of vocations.

HEALTH

Your selection of this card suggests a projected personality through whom you vicariously experienced one or more incarnations during which you were primarily engaged in attempting to do good to others in this way. You may perhaps have known an existence as a medical priest/ priestess in a healing temple or even have played the role of "barefoot doctor" or physician to the poor, who received little material return for all the good you managed to do.

In the course of frequent contact with the sick and dying as a career in the healing professions, you may have experienced great depths of emotion, from profound despair and helplessness, to joy, love and a sense of accomplishment through being able actually to alleviate suffering. An incarnation in the persona of such an apparent individual presents many opportunities both to advance in one's own understanding and to better the condition of others. Witnessing first hand, on a continuing basis, the many ills and the fragility of the physical body confers an insight into the fleeting nature of the physical world.

The seemingly inevitable deterioration of the physical form always provides an opportunity to experience directly the transitory nature both of human life and of the apparent physical world itself. These penetrating insights into humankind as a whole and their essential place in the universal consciousness have left a lasting impression. In contemplating these possibilities, resonances are bound to arise.

5. EDUCATION

Your selection of this card suggests that, through an emanated personality, you experienced one or more incarnations during which you were in some way associated with the field of education, either as teacher or as student. You are likely to have psychically retained many such experiences from what you perceive to be both the past and the future, as well as in your current apparent incarnation.

EDUCATION

All people are life-long, habitual students whether or not it is clear to them. Incarnate life is wholly and entirely a learning process. All that you have, by proxy, experienced or will ever experience in "time" is, from the individual entity's point of view, a search for ultimate truth. It is sad that modern education is apparently locked into a materialist view that everything is relative and that, accordingly, there is, and can be, no absolute truth. It has thereby blocked itself, and countless earnest, promising students, from achieving the supreme insight into the true nature both of themselves and of this "God"-dreamed universe.

Teaching as the conveying of one's knowledge to others is a noble calling — and one which may be peculiarly rich in reincarnational memories to be recaptured. This is particularly true of spiritual teaching in a guru–disciple relationship like that of the Master Jesus and his closest followers.

AGRICULTURE

6. AGRICULTURE

For thousands of years, the agricultural laborer and the yeoman have been the rock-solid basis for the development of virtually every society. Without them there could have been no progress beyond the hunting and gathering culture of very early prehistoric and protohistoric times, and without them today we could not physically survive.

During the long course of your apparent sojourn on this planet, through the manifold personalities that you have appeared to emanate and to project into incarnation, you have vicariously experienced countless lifetimes in a rural environment where you were more or less closely tied to the soil. An important part of your activity had to do with animal husbandry.

A particular advantage of incarnation in this environment would have been your closeness to nature. You experienced strong feelings in the course of observing the growth and decay of vegetation, the breeding and nurturing of animals, the sun, the wind, the rain and the change of the seasons. All of these elemental experiences had a profound effect on you.

Life in a rural setting could have been rather dull and unexciting, although physically challenging. In that context, if undisturbed by outside forces like war or revolution, a relatively calm, unruffled existence may not have generated many notable memories that are readily recoverable from the psyche, although your entire history, down to the finest detail, is nevertheless fully accessible to you.

7. ARTIST ~ ARTISAN

ARTIST~ARTISAN

Humankind have been creative from the very beginning of their presence on this planet. Much of this creative urge has been channeled into works of fine art such as painting, sculpture and other expressions of an innate skill. Included in this occupational group are the artist, the writer, the composer, the singer, and the skilled player of musical instruments. The architect and craftsmen of all kinds fall into this vast category.

Your selection of this card suggests an enormous number of possible activities that you have experienced through your various projected personalities.

The psychic memories of such experiences are often far more readily accessible to your current egoic consciousness because they reflect *inborn* tendencies that are carried over from one seeming incarnation to another. While this is outstandingly clear in the case of a Mozart, it is equally true, if less obviously so, for countless other, if outwardly less-gifted artists.

To gain access to memories of such a vicarious experience in other embodiments, it would be helpful if you were to attempt to examine closely such inborn artistic talents as you are currently aware of in the present incarnation, and try earnestly and continually to trace them to their source.

8

BUILDER

8. BUILDER

In the course of their several long climbs back to civilization during intervals between catastophes, humans have been forced to build and to rebuild so as to ensure their survival as a species. Beyond the call of necessity, builders have often been inspired to erect temples of various kinds to express their religious feelings.

The profession of the mason, the worker in stone, dates from the earliest times. Some of the most remarkable, indeed incomprehensible, achievements include the Trilithon at the so-called Temple of Jupiter-Helios at Baalbek, the ageless Sphinx, the Great ("Khufu") Pyramid at Giza, and the Oseirion at Abydos. The Trilithon and the Great Pyramid are described as "incomprehensible" simply because human beings of the present day are incapable either of explaining how they were constructed or of themselves re-creating them. The Great Pyramid and the lesser Khafra and Menkaura Pyramids at Giza are masterpieces of precision engineering of a staggering sophistication that bespeaks the existence of an extraordinarily high technology among the very ancient Egyptians. Other examples of extraordinary buildings such as Carnac, Stonehenge, Callanish and Tiwanaku reveal the existence of an ancient but astronomically sophisticated, worldwide megalithic civilization. The almost miraculous stone walls of Sacsayhuaman and Ollantaytambo in Peru can only be marvelled at.

On a more modest level, humans have built homes, whether mundane or grand, in all varieties of climate from the mildest to the most severe. Even when living in caves, they made changes to the caves as well as decorating them.

Your selection of this card suggests an experience through one or more of your projected incarnate personalities in construction and engineering activities. Indeed your participation in such work is certain. All human beings are or have been builders of one thing or another from the very beginning of their appearance on this planet.

Your study of such great past works of engineering and building as the Great Pyramid and of the engineering problems posed by the quarrying and erection of the Trilithon should help to rekindle your memories of lifetimes in which you apparently were, or will be, directly involved in similar activities.

9

TRADER

9. TRADER

As the unquestionably genuine ancient maps most undeniably show, the world was widely known to humankind, at the latest, at the peak of the last (Wisconsin) Ice Age, seventeen thousand years BP ("before the present"). It is impossible to know how much earlier anatomically modern human beings were acquainted with the geography of the Earth in detail, but there is evidence that such knowledge extends much farther back in time than conventional anthropology is prepared even to consider.

People make maps in order, above all, first to explore and then to trade. The role of the traveling merchant is one of the very oldest. For trade to grow, ever-better maps are required by a sea-going culture that does not view the ocean as a barrier, as does a "land-lubber," but as a highway. Ocean-going vessels date from earliest times, back to Atlantis and beyond. For at least one hundred thousand years such ships have crossed and recrossed the oceans, distributing goods and redistributing populations that, in a typically human way, were continually on the move in search of greater opportunity. The trading vessel played a major role in these multifarious activities, protohistoric, prehistoric and modern.

Your choice of this card bespeaks any number of embodied personalities through which you have appeared to experience life as a merchant or trader of one kind or another, with possibly a bit of piracy as the opportunity presented itself! These were exciting lives of danger and adventure that certainly made a great impact on you at the psychic level. If you pay close attention, such resonances are sure to arise.

10. LABORER

All lives involve labor of one sort or another, heavy or light, physical or mental. From the humble street peddler or shopkeeper to the director of a great commercial enterprise, people have always worked both to create and then to exchange goods and services with each other, to their mutual benefit.

Some laboring work is more menial, that is at least apparently more degrading or servile, than others. Nevertheless, without exception there is dignity in all labor-intensive occupa-

10

LABORER

tions; they are hence worthy of the greatest respect and consideration. Parasitic fops who sneer at and look down on the laborer or small businessperson, who ultimately support them in their idle luxury, display only crass ignorance of the true value of things.

Your selection of this card suggests that you have passed any number of projected incarnations in honest toil. All people have undergone such experiences many times. It may even be said that incarnate life in the personality is itself nothing but a laborious effort to achieve a return to the One Source. This is the most important work of all.

Every single incarnation contains a valuable lesson or lessons directed to this end. Do not hesitate to record in your journal any and all labor-associated psychic resonances.

11. BEGGAR

This card depicts the apparently, but not necessarily, unfortunate existence that has been the lot of many an incarnate personality at one time or another. What you appeared to experience through your projected personality in that situation may very possibly have left a trace on the psyche that is now readily available for recall.

11

BEGGAR

The beggar is normally driven to ply his or her trade by dire poverty. Yet there are those who make a virtue of necessity by becoming a professional, like the legendary Jewish *shnorrer*, who considers himself to be a fully respectable member of an occupational group — a man so bold as to demand his alms as a matter of right. Another type of professional beggar is to be seen in poor countries, where children may even be deliberately maimed in order to be exhibited so as to excite the pity of passers-by.

The beggar of this card is not one of those. This is the true beggar who has been driven to this activity because no other course was open to him or her except death by starvation. Malnourished, chronically ill, shivering from the cold or burned by the sun, shunned by all self-styled "good" people, the beggar endured much and learned much from this most instructive and ultimately beneficial embodiment.

12

COURTESAN

12. COURTESAN

Whether in the highest civilization or the most primitive, the world's oldest profession has always been with us. At practically all times and in virtually all cultures, female and male prostitutes are to be found. It may come as a surprise to some to be assured that there is actually nothing particularly reprehensible in this, or indeed in any human activity. It must frankly be recognized that people have been forced to do all sorts of things to make a living even in the most prosperous times. And times can be very hard indeed.

Your past or present apparent association with the activities of prostitutes, whether as whore, catamite, pander or customer, is more likely than most are readily prepared to admit. In more enlightened societies, the role of the courtesan is treated with the respect and consideration for the natural rights of the individual that it honestly deserves.

Your selection of this card suggests, through your emanated personality, including possibly the current incarnation, your association to some extent with some aspect of this unfairly much-maligned occupation.

As the physical expression of one's sexual urges evokes the most basic, foundational elements of the physical transmission of life from generation to generation, you may well have acquired some readily accessible psychic marks of such activity. If there are resonances to this effect, try not to reject them, but to accept them with an open mind, and to record them in your journal as faithfully as you can.

Nothing that is human is alien to you.

13. MOTHER

Motherhood is something that all have experienced, regardless of present gender. This card represents an incarnation in which there were many opportunities to feel both the great joys and the deep sorrows of a mother.

The female who undergoes the experience of bearing a child is connected to the cycles of nature in a way vastly different from that of the male. As it is the female who gives birth, it is she who has the primal relationship with nature. Among other things, she is provided with a remarkable memory lapse. A partial veil of forgetfulness is mercifully laid over what is usually the painful birth of a baby. There are parallels to this in your own forgetfulness of other projected embodiments and in the pain you constantly, if unconsciously, experience through your separation from the Source. When you are ready, this boundary thins down and can be pierced by a perceptive and intuitive awareness that is no longer confined by the circumstances of your present apparent embodiment.

One bears a heavy burden of responsibility if one chooses to devote oneself to others in the role of a mother. With loving parents, a child is nurtured and supported in unconditional love. Selflessly to release and to allow one's offspring to make his or her own life decisions, without judgment, provides an opportunity to learn the lesson of detachment. Still, the idyllic unconditional love of a parent is not always fulfilled. This card may trigger a memory of abandonment and rejection, as either child or parent.

This card is an invitation to explore the incarnation experience with particular emphasis on family relationships in your current or other emanated personalities.

Associations from other apparent embodiments often manifest in families. It is more than likely that you have in this way known members of your current family. Although the experience may be troublesome, the many possibilities inherent in shared familial relationships add greatly to the understanding of life. As a family appears to evolve and to mature with the seeming passage of time, it may become ever more obvious that, in truth, this life experience is no more than a passing dream.

14. RELIGIOUS

RELIGIOUS

Through many of your projected personalities, you have pursued a religious vocation. The very fact that you have been drawn to using these cards is, in itself, proof of your continuing interest in spiritual development in a quest that has extended over many apparent lifetimes.

In pursuit of self-realization you have appeared to project personalities into many times and environments, now as a monk or priest, then as a nun or priestess. In the apparent course of those projections you have vicariously endured many hardships in your outward search for that which can be found in its unlimited fullness only within.

At the end of your long, long quest, you find that only by transcending every projected personality is it possible to achieve insight into ultimate reality, by *seeing through* that which changes into the changeless *That* which lies under the appearance of the world.

Be patient. Your devoted search for religious and philosophic truth will not be in vain. Continue to seek within. Enter the present moment and fill yourself with silence.

○ CULTURE CARDS — INTRODUCTION

As discussed in Chapter Four, *Human Origins*, the earliest periods of human activity on this planet remain largely unknown, due in part to the success of Establishment scientists in either simply ignoring or deliberately suppressing evidence, however persuasive, that does not fit in with their hypotheses. Much of what is enshrined in textbooks is at best incomplete. The modern, accepted picture of human beings having evolved from ape-like creatures only a couple of hundred thousand years ago is increasingly seen to be inadequate.

This is not to say that the doctrine of physical evolution is necessarily wrong. It will, however, require profound modification. The idea that we are all descended from one African ancestor does not stand in the face of evidence that recognizably human beings, whether or not directly ancestral in the biological sense, have been present on this planet for many millions of years. For over a century, so-called "OOPARTS," out-of-place artifacts, from geological strata millions, even hundreds of millions of years old, have been found, identified as to time and place of origin, then conveniently forgotten, as they did not fit into the current scientific paradigm of a steady evolution by chance involving a process called natural selection leading to the survival of the fittest over vast periods of time, with modern humans suddenly arriving on the scene a mere thirty-five thousand to forty thousand years ago.

Artifacts left by earlier humans on this planet have been identified on Manitoulin Island in Canada (125,000 years), at Hueyatlaco, Mexico (250,000 years) and at Table Mountain, California (from nine million to fifty-five million years BP). Similar OOPARTS have been found in many, many locations, testifying to the presence of recognizably human or humanoid forerunners on this planet as early as the Mesozoic Era that ended sixty-five million years ago. This cohabitation with dinosaurs is clearly suggested by the ICA stones of Peru and the Acámbaro figures of Mexico.

The truth is that very little can be said with certainty about our forebears. Hundreds if not thousands of cultures have come and gone. Only a very few of those that are known to us can be covered in these seventeen cards. Hence these Culture cards represent just some of the civilizations that have cycled through the rise and the seemingly inevitable decline of collective human societies. Every experience of the triumph or defeat of a culture adds greatly to one's growth. Associations and memories of particular cultures are rendered more easily accessible in the case of a shared group experience. You no doubt will also find that you are already aware of intuitive resonances to certain regions.

These cards are designed to stimulate further these far memories so that you may develop a greater understanding both of the illusory nature of this physical world and, ultimately, of who you really are.

15. PREHISTORIC

This card relates to an early period of human physical evolution. It includes a possible lifetime as what has become known to anthropology as the Palaeolithic and Neolithic periods. These Old and New Stone Age peoples included offshoots such as Homo Erectus, Homo Neanderthalensis, Homo Habilis, and the allegedly more directly ancestral Magdalenian, Aurignacian, Cro-Magnon type.

During these periods, circumstances were far from ideal. Life was often difficult and extremely dangerous. You had to cope with all sorts of hazards to protect yourself and your loved ones. Enormous cave bears, dire wolves and sabre-toothed cats were an ever-present danger. Any crippling injury could prove fatal. Those were desperate times, when people had to depend on each other, that made a deep impression on you, some sort of memory of which you may well have carried over into the present apparent incarnation. Such experiences can leave deep emotional scars that enable one more readily to identify another person or persons, from that earlier period, in the current life situation.

Surviving remnants of superb cave paintings, such as those found in Australia and France dated to thirty thousand to forty thousand years ago, are indications of societies that greatly valued artistic expression. These traces of creative artwork may provide you with an access point to explore more fully the role of these early ancestors in our little-known human history.

It may surprise you to see that the card shows a human being coexisting with dinosaurs. According to the scientistic Establishment, the dinosaurs were completely wiped out some sixty-five million years ago by an asteroid or comet strike off the coast of Yucatan, an event which is said to have occurred long before the emergence of the first humanoids. There is compelling evidence that anatomically modern human beings actually did coexist with dinosaurs, either before or since the formal end of the Mesozoic Era, and have left the proof of such cohabitation in many places, particularly in South America.

There have been many occasions in the past when a high civilization has been destroyed by a catastrophic event. No one has ever been able to establish, with any certainty, when modern-type human beings first arrived on this planet, although conventional archaeology offers many unproven hypotheses.

16. PROTOHISTORIC

Protohistoric culture arose later than and ran parallel to the *prehistoric* culture, in the same way in which technologically advanced

16

PROTOHISTORIC

societies today still coexist with simple, tribal cultures elsewhere in the world.

The period covered here is from approximately 200,000 BCE to the sudden catastrophic end of the last Ice Age about 9600 BCE. The Greenland glacier ice cores point to 9645 BCE as the most likely year in which this event took place. At that time the low-lying Atlantean civilization was destroyed either by a Near Earth Object (NEO) strike in the Atlantic Ocean or by the passing of a massive NEO whose gravity moved the oceans from their basins. The traumatized remnants of humankind, those fortunate enough to have escaped the Great Deluge that ensued, reduced once again to unlettered barbarism, eventually came down from the mountains to start the climb back to civilization all over again. Survivors found their way to Egypt and Sumer in the East and to the Americas in the West where, with earlier colonists to those areas, they gave birth to new civilizations that led eventually to our own.

A previous protohistoric civilization, the forerunner of Atlantis, was based on a large land area, now largely submerged in the Pacific Ocean. There, on a continent known as "Mu" or "Lemuria" to occultists and so-called channelers or as

"Sundaland" or "Pacifica" to modern geologists, humankind are said to have originated. This was allegedly a very remote period of high civilization. The Indians are said to have originated there. The Sumerians are believed to have come from the same Pacific area, having moved west, via India, to present-day Iraq when their Pacific Ocean homeland was destroyed. The Hopi "Native Americans" of the Southwestern USA also claim to have come from there, fleeing from a Great Flood, untold ages ago.

The earliest evidences of anatomically modern humans in the known world are to be found not in Africa, as currently proclaimed, but in Southern California, and along the west coast of South America, dating back to as early as three hundred to five hundred thousand years BP. This is far earlier than they appeared in Africa or in Europe and, indeed, earlier even than the supposed emergence of the Neanderthals. The Native Americans of eastern North America arrived much later, having traveled west from Atlantis, which was also the home of the Cro-Magnons who, it is alleged, *suddenly* appeared in Western Europe about thirty-five thousand to forty thousand years ago, alongside the Neanderthals who had dominated the area for perhaps one hundred thousand years.

Memories forged in these times may provide a more holistic view of the complex but not yet fully understood history of our species. Drawing this card is a call to meditate on the many unknowns of our history. Discover through your own intuitive research the mysterious origins of our early ancestors, memories of which are accessible to you.

MESOPOTAMIA

17. MESOPOTAMIA

The Sumerians claimed a history of 241,200 years after "kingship descended from heaven." This is where Oannes the fish/man/god, the leader of a group of *Seven Sages*, is said to have brought the arts and civilization to Sumer from the stars. This area is present-day Iraq, home to the ancient, but highly cultivated peoples of Sumer, Akkad and, later, Babylonia.

According to one legend, the "black-headed" Sumerians originally migrated from a drowned land in the farthest East. They established themselves in a fertile valley that is now at the bottom of the Persian/Arab Gulf. Their first and the oldest of five antediluvian cities was Eridu, allegedly dating back almost a quarter of a million years. The original Eridu is now submerged, together with the other four lost ancient cities, Badtibira, Larak, Sippar and Shurrupak. These ancient cities were drowned as a consequence of the Great Deluge of about 9600 BCE, a world-wide series of storms, earthquakes and tsunamis caused by either the impact or the close passage of a massive Near Earth Object (NEO) and the associated abrupt melting of the ice dams that had held back vast glacial lakes, thereby bringing the last Ice Age and its associated high civilization to a sudden, catastrophic end.

In Sumer, according to legend, An, or Anu, the sky father, god of all gods, took over heaven when it was separated from Earth (Ki). His consort, the Sky Goddess Nammu, was "the mother who gave birth to heaven and earth." Other gods, the Annunaku (Igigi), included Ea (Enki), Lord of Wisdom, tutelary deity of protohistoric Eridu, Enlil, Ninhursaga the "Creatrix," Inanna/Ishtar Queen of Heaven, Ninlil, Ninurta/Marduk, Nergal, Nanna, Ningirsu, Lahar, Uttu, Utu/Shamash, Dumuzi, the demon god Pazuzu, Sin and Ereshkigal, Queen of the Underworld, among many others in a complex pantheon.

The first Creation story was recorded here, antedating the biblical version by thousands of years. These gods, the "Anuna" or "Annunaku of heaven and earth," are said to have created *homo sapiens sapiens,* or modern humans in their present form, by genetic modification, using earlier, proto-human species as their raw material.

The early Mesopotamians were great astronomers, fully aware of the size and planetary configuration of the solar system, with the sun at its center. They reported a "war in the heavens" between planets, one of which, called "Tiamat," was reduced to the asteroid belt that now lies between Mars and Jupiter; an event that led to a Great Deluge.

Here the Biblical Flood legend originated. Here is where Gilgamesh, King of Uruk, in search of immortality, sought and

found the Sumerian prototype of the biblical Noah, Ziusura/
Utnapishtim, the savior of humankind and the immortal
survivor of the Deluge.

After the Great Flood, "kingship was reestablished." Many
cities were built higher up the valleys of the Tigris and Euphrates
rivers, including three that were nostalgically given the names of
ancient drowned cities: Eridu, Sippar and Shurrupak. Other cities
later established included Ugarit, Harran, Uruk, Nineveh, Nippur,
Nimrud, Elam, Mari, Erech, Borsippa, Kish, Ashur, Susa, Agash,
Larsa, Umma, Basra, Agade, Ur, Adab, Nisrab and Zabalam.

The Mesopotamian was a long, long period of protohistory.
When you draw this card, you open a door to a vast, mysterious
past. Try to feel if any of the names of these cities and "gods"
resonate with you. Any such resonances should be meditated on
and any recovered memories should be carefully recorded and
thought about deeply and often.

18. EGYPT

Egypt is a mysterious civilization, with many anomalies not yet
understood or explained satisfactorily by mainstream researchers.
The immense temples of antiquity are monuments that testify
not only to the extraordinary technical skills of this culture, but
also to an unique understanding of sacred geometry. This was an
extremely high civilization from very early times, dating back to
about thirty-nine thousand years BP, according to native

Egyptian historians, whose testimony has, typically, been ignored by modern Egyptologists. The early migrants into Egypt brought with them a very high technology that enabled them and their successors eventually to construct the Giza Pyramids, the Valley and the Sphinx Temples, the Oseirion at Abydos and the Great Sphinx itself. Egypt's *Seven Sages* are said to have come from an island, having survived a catastrophic flood. The greatest cultural influ-

ences came from these "Atlanteans," who had already established colonies in Egypt long millennia before the destruction of their homeland in about 9600 BCE. They left clear evidence of an almost incredible ability to work in stone. They demonstrably not only employed sophisticated tools to machine the limestone and granite of the Great (Khufu) Pyramid to the finest tolerances but also left clear signs, telltale scars in the stone, of having used lathes and ultrasonic machining methods (see Bibliography B: Dunn).

The extraordinary antiquity of the Egyptian civilization has been established on geological evidence that clearly demonstrates that the Sphinx and its enclosure, as well as the associated Sphinx and Valley Temples, are vastly older than establishment Egyptology is prepared to admit (see Bibliography B: West).

In addition, the Nabta Playa stone alignments in the remote desert west of Abu Simbel, dating from as early as eleven thousand years BCE or even earlier, display an extraordinary knowledge of astronomy among the very early Egyptians, who obviously knew the phenomenon of precession of the equinoxes, both the size and the oblate spheroid shape of the Earth, the place of the sun in the solar system and the place of the solar system in the Milky Way Galaxy. The Nabta Playa alignments indicate the direction and the actual relative distances of a number of major stars as can be deduced from their ready convertibility into light-years (see Bibliography B: Brophy).

Egyptian wisdom was always considered by other cultures as antedating and inspiring their own philosophies and sciences. It was there that Solon, in about 600 BCE, learned the story of Atlantis from Egyptian priests. Pythagoras, Plato and other seekers spent some years there to obtain initiation into the Mysteries.

The long, long history of Egypt suggests that your emanated personalities have apparently sojourned there for any number of incarnations. The very length of this period and its remarkable accomplishments account for the fascination virtually all people feel with respect to Egypt.

This is the counsel bequeathed to you by the Egyptian Ger-Maa, Amen-em-Apt, who flourished during the reign of the "Sun" Pharaoh, Amenhotep the Magnificent, in the fourteenth century BCE:

Canst thou forget thyself while sitting?
Seat thyself in the arms of God.
Fill thyself full of silence.
Thou shalt find the Life.

19. GREECE

This card covers the period from the pre-Socratic philosophers in about 600 BCE to the last of the neo-Platonists, with the savage murder of Hypatia in Alexandria by fanatical Christian monks in the year 415 CE, at the behest of the Patriarch Cyril.

This Hellenistic culture was the most enlightened in the entire recorded history of modern western civilization; a tolerant, open, democratic society in which no one could be persecuted for private religious or philosophical beliefs and in which most were left free, and were even encouraged, to think for themselves and to seek wisdom and knowledge in their own way.

This was a time in which the Mystery Schools flourished. The most prominent statesmen and philosophers of antiquity sought initiation into these schools, the products of which thereafter were famous for leading the most exemplary lives. Successful initiation normally included the elicitation of memories of past incarnations and, on occasion, may have conferred a personal, direct insight into cosmic consciousness.

While the ancient practice of slavery persisted, a meritorious slave could earn his or her freedom, especially from an enlightened master or mistress.

The height of Greek philosophy may be said to be enshrined in the inscription:

$$\text{"}\Gamma N\Omega\Theta I \ \Sigma E \ AYTON\text{"}$$

"KNOW THYSELF," embossed on the lintel of the temple of Apollo at Delphi.

The longer and even more illuminating version of this injunction is:

"Know Thyself and thou wilt know the Universe and the Gods."

If you fully comprehend its meaning, you will finally understand the ultimate purpose of these *Reincarnation Cards*.

20. ROME

Following the conquest of Greece by the Romans, the classical Greek and Roman civilizations became fused. As Greece was absorbed into the Roman Empire, Greek philosophers, physicians and other teachers were much prized by the ruder Romans, who took full advantage of their availability as a conquered people, to soften and to humanize their own more primitive ways. Well-born Romans, as children, were frequently taught by highly educated Greek slaves. The Roman Emperor Claudius, for example, actually wrote his memoirs in Greek rather than in Latin. From Greek philosophy, the Romans imbibed the most

20

ROME

just and liberal notions of the dignity of human nature and the characteristics of a truly civilized society.

The basic Roman character itself, however, was militaristic and aggressive. It later degenerated into domination by a "bread and circuses" policy devised by the Caesars. This was aimed at the pacification and control of the increasingly unruly, bloodthirsty mob, who actually rejoiced to see the slaughter of people in the arena. The Romans' attitude toward those whom they conquered is well expressed by the words put into the mouth of the British chieftain Calgacus by the historian Tacitus, in the *Agricola:*

> *Ubi solitudinem faciunt, pacem appellant.*
> *Where they make a wilderness, they call it peace.*

Also condemned by Calgacus as "plunderers of the known world in the false name of empire," the Romans were nevertheless great engineers who built aqueducts and roads that are still in use today. They were also great law-givers who laid the foundations of all modern Western legal systems.

Roman history was long and bloody. The Republic and Empire lasted close to a thousand years in the West, while the Eastern Roman, or Byzantine Empire, based in Constantinople, lasted another thousand years until it was finally extinguished only as late as the fifteenth century CE.

Details of your apparent incarnations during this dynamic, colorful period, should be more readily accessible to you than experiences of a quieter, less stimulating era.

21. DARK AGES

The Graeco-Roman period was one of high civilization. With the rise of Christianity, however, especially after it was made the State religion by decree of the Roman Emperor Constantine I ("The Great,") a period of intellectual, spiritual and economic stagnation ensued.

Earlier, many philosophies circulated freely in a mutually tolerant intellectual atmosphere; an enlightened period when people were free to think independently and to seek their own salvation in their own way. With the steady rise of Christianity to a dominant position, all of this was to change. Not only the pagan temples but most of the architectural wonders of the Graeco-Roman world were deliberately destroyed and left in ruins. All were to be forced to accept one body of religious teachings devised by a hierarchy of men who were devoted primarily to maintaining and enhancing their wealth and their temporal power over others. Any who chose to think freely for themselves were to be condemned for the "crime" of heresy,

21

DARK AGES

defined as the holding of an opinion contrary to Christian doctrine as laid down by the Church (from the Greek *hairesis*, free choice or opinion). Accordingly, to be a freethinker was to be a criminal. Consequently, for a thousand years, Europe was sunk in the Dark Ages, a period characterized by ignorance, fear, a vast poverty of mind and spirit; an era of widespread barbarism during which such knowledge as had been preserved was either locked up in the monasteries or openly studied only by the relatively enlightened Arabs, to whose careful preservation of at least some part of antique knowledge Europe owes so much.

These were harsh years in the West. Warfare was forever being waged between one small group or tribe and its neighbors.

The roads were unsafe. Robbery, rape and murder were common crimes. If one was wise, one ventured out only when necessary. One was forced to work long and hard simply in order to survive in an illiterate, largely subsistence society. Surpluses were stolen by local petty chieftains, or "lords." Yet, such is the resilience of the human spirit, there were periods when life could be made bearable.

Your apparent incarnation at this time could have been very harsh, or even relatively pleasant. Your memories of such lawless times as these are probably closer to the surface of your current personal consciousness than are those of a more tranquil era.

22

CELTIC

22. CELTIC

The Celts, although to be found everywhere, are an all but unknown race. Although by "Keltoi," the ancient Greeks meant any northern "barbarians," the range of the Celtic peoples extended from the Taklamakan Desert on the borders of China in the east, through southern Europe north of Greece and Italy, to Switzerland, France, Ireland and Scotland in the west. Known to the Romans as the Gauls, today they are deemed to include the Bretons in France, and the Cornish, Welsh, Irish, Scottish and Manx peoples of Britain, all united by a common bond of cognate languages and deeply held mystic traditions.

Wherever they came from, these western Celts are closely bound up with Druidism, the origin of which is cloaked in an even greater mystery. Legend has it that a tribe of enlightened prophets, sages and philosophers, the Tuatha de Danann, came to Ireland from Atlantis just prior to its destruction in about 9600 BCE. Having driven out or absorbed the earlier inhabitants, the Firbolgs and Fomors, they were, in turn, invaded but only partly subdued by so-called "Milesian" Celts in about 2000 BCE.

Over the centuries, the Celts absorbed much of the Druidic philosophy and became "versed in the knowledge of the Tuatha de Danann." The Druids were fully aware of the actuality of reincarnation. They were also conscious of other worlds parallel to this one; worlds in which time has lost its conventional meaning, where a day can pass in a moment or last for a hundred of our years.

They built numerous mounds, but few temples, and they congregated in sacred glades in the forest. There they meditated and communed with the universal nature spirit that forever lies under the seen. The Great Mother Earth and the Invincible Sun were regarded as the source of all Life.

The sexes were treated as absolutely equal. From the earliest times, female warriors fought alongside their men at the very forefront of battles. Originally matriarchal, Celtic society became male-dominated only after Roman Christianity replaced the Celtic Church, which had retained strong links to its Druidic heritage.

The unique blend of the Celts with the Tuatha de Danann is still manifest today in the peculiar psychic abilities of the various western Celtic peoples as inspired and spread by the Druids of Britain. The true Celtic culture is enshrouded by an aura of magic and mystery. The Celtic world is one in which virtually anything can and indeed often does happen — where the diaphanous veil between the worlds can become transparent and the intervening walls fall away.

Your projected personality in this culture at any stage of its wild and romantic history has left a deep and lasting impression on your psyche. Seek it again in the stillness of silent communion with nature.

23. RENAISSANCE

The rebirth of European civilization began in Florence under the Medicis, particularly Cosimo (1389–1464 CE) and his grandson, Lorenzo The Magnificent (1449–1492 CE) who charged Marsilio Ficino (1433–1499 CE), translator and promulgator of Plato's teaching, and others with seeking out and rescuing the classical Greek writings that had long been lost to the West.

The Renaissance owed much to the fall of Constantinople, the capital of the Eastern Roman Empire, to the Turks in the year 1453 CE. This apparent disaster for the West generated a new, larger influx of educated Greeks into Italy as refugees. Their presence in Italy provided an immense stimulus to the general intellectual rebirth that was char-

RENAISSANCE

acteristic of this period. This opened the way to the growth of an intellectual freedom from the dictates of an unenlightened religious hierarchy, a liberation that is still not completely achieved.

Greek scholars, fleeing from the Turks, had brought thousands of Greek manuscripts to Italy even before the fall of Constantinople in 1453 CE. Earlier still, in 1204 CE, a Franco-Venetian crusader fleet captured and looted Constantinople and for sixty years thereafter, Italians had access to the great libraries there, although regrettably, much was destroyed by fire at the time of the invasion.

The Renaissance, literally the "Rebirth," was an era of explosive intellectual growth as well as expansion in the arts, centered in, but by no means limited to, Italy. This was also a period of great turmoil. Many minor wars were constantly being fought between cities and petty principalities. This period also saw the gradual break-up of the feudal system, the spread of literacy with the independent invention of movable type by Johann Gutenberg (1398–1468 CE), the progressive liberation of the peasants from servitude and the growth both of a mercantilist class and of the towns.

This was an exciting, colorful and dangerous time that undoubtedly left its mark on your individual psyche. This may well provide you with access to apparent lives associated with this time, giving you an opportunity, once more, the better to understand your true nature.

24. ISLAMIC

The spread of Islam since the death of the Holy Prophet Muhammad has embraced many countries and submerged many other religious cultures. Unlike most other faiths, Islam is an entire way of life. Its holy book, the Qur'an, pronounces on virtually every aspect of social intercourse. Consequently, from a Western point of view, the position of a woman in Islamic cultures can be experienced as narrow and restrictive. Your vicarious experience in an Islamic culture may have been a traumatic one as a female, a slave, or both. Experiences like these leave a deep impression on the psyche that can easily resurface in a later embodiment in the form of a phobia or a particular personal characteristic.

Early Islamic society was steeped in violence. Islam was born in battle and spread by the sword, driving the peaceful Buddhism from large parts of Asia and leaving its lasting fingerprints in the Balkans of southeastern Europe. Modern Western civilization, nevertheless, owes much to the preservation in Islamic societies of many ancient

24

ISLAMIC

literary works and philosophical treatises that had been lost to the West in the Dark Ages, during which it labored and suffered under a Roman Christian tyranny that has left its own scars on the human psyche.

Today, there is much in the Islamic culture to be admired. Your selection of this card may stimulate buried memories of an incarnation of great beauty, characterized by a lofty spirituality expressed in philosophy and poetry.

Islam, like the cognate Arabic words Muslim and Salaam, implies peaceful surrender to the divine will, the utter acceptance of that which *is*. Such an unreserved acceptance by one who has wholly and completely *resigned,* supported by a total faith in and confidence of support by a higher power, leads to complete inner freedom and to the "peace that passeth understanding;" a resignation reflected in the Arabic, "Kulli shayy fi yid allah" or "All things are in the hands of God."

25

INDIA~SOUTHEAST ASIA

25. INDIA ~ SOUTHEAST ASIA

Your selection of this card suggests a connection to a culture that gave birth to the highest philosophy. In India, more than in any other country on Earth, the traditions of an ancient great world civilization are preserved. Contemporary with Atlantis, ancient India has the longest-lived continuous period of civilization on the planet.

This extraordinarily ancient culture goes back many, many thousands of years into prehistoric and protohistoric times. Memory of this civilization has been all but totally obscured by catastrophic events, such as earthquakes, volcanic eruptions with vast lava flows, and flooding, involving the cataclysmic subsidence of whole cities to below sea level long, long ago. The remains of huge built-up areas are to be seen beneath the sea off the coasts of present-day India and Sri Lanka, evidence of civilization dating back tens of thousands of years.

The still-undeciphered writings found at Mohenjo-Daro in present-day Pakistan are remarkably similar to the "rongo-rongo" writing of Easter Island far away across the Pacific Ocean, as well as to inscriptions found in Brazil. This is clear evidence of a very widespread, extremely ancient civilization. South Asians long ago reached Central and South America and exercised a great influence in the development of civilization in those areas.

The antiquity of Indian culture extends far back into protohistory, to the legendary period of the destruction of "Mu"/"Lemuria"/Pacifica/Sundaland, in a series of cataclysms that extended over two hundred thousand years. Survivors of great cataclysms from about 200,000 to 50,000 BCE fled eastward to what is now South America, westward to Southeast Asia, the Indian sub-continent, and as far as Sumer and Egypt in protohistoric times. As with Sumer and Egypt, a group of *Seven Sages* preserved ancient Indian knowledge through the several cataclysms, including the last Great Deluge of about 9600 BCE.

Indian history affords an example of the unwillingness of Establishment scientists to consider seriously the history of the country as related by the people themselves, who tell of a highly civilized Indian Empire that was destroyed in a great war involving aerial vehicles and what appear to have been nuclear weapons, as recorded in the *Ramayana* and the *Mahabharata*.

The *Rg Veda* speaks of a still earlier, far more remote period, when the Indians' ancestors came from over the sea as survivors of a great flood, or Deluge, the Flood of Manu, that destroyed an incredibly ancient civilization, presumably that centered in the Pacific Ocean region.

26

CHINA~JAPAN

26. CHINA ~ JAPAN

Chinese civilization has been shaped over the centuries by the "Three Teachings," those of Kung Fu Tze (Confucius), Lao Tze and Fo (Buddha). Of these, only the first two are native to China, and of those, only that of Lao Tze is a profoundly mystical philosophy. Originating in India, Chinese "Ch'an" Buddhism later moved to Japan, where it became known as "Zen."

Confucianism concentrates on the values of human relationships. In effect, it is a code of conduct based on a moral sense of social and political order through the cultivation of rituals and music.

The Chinese character depicted on the card, Tao, or the "Way" is primarily associated with Lao Tze. Shown seated on his ox, he wrote the "Book of Tao" while on his way to retirement in the northwestern mountains. Unlike Confucianism, the Tao is a clear guide to the highest Self-realization. It is truly a "Way."

Much earlier, however, extensive Chinese explorations of America ("Fu-Sang") were conducted in the twenty-third century BCE and by Buddhist missionaries, in the fifth century CE. Over the centuries, thousands of Chinese actually emigrated to the Americas in pre-Columbian times. The Chinese influence on the people and cultures of the Americas is both obvious and profound, as is clearly demonstrated by the statuary of Central America and the existence of ancient, detailed Chinese maps of "Fu Sang" that are more than four thousand years old.

Your projected incarnation into this civilization at any level may be indicative of a high degree of spirituality, depending upon the other cards selected.

This card may also refer to an apparent incarnation in the ancient, highly advanced Jomon civilization that flourished in Japan and the Ryukyu Islands of that country as long ago as the year 15,000 BCE. This culture was largely inundated subsequently by a Great Deluge that there, as elsewhere, left only a relatively few survivors. Some of the submerged structures of this culture have recently been explored in the seas off Japan and Taiwan (see Bibliography B: Hancock). Traces of the Japanese Jomon culture have also been found as far away as Ecuador. The early Jomon, and also the modern so-called "Yayoi" Japanese, greatly influenced the development of Central American civilization.

These very early cultures have protohistoric links with the ancient Pacific Ocean continental civilization known to occultists as "Lemuria" or "Mu," the original cradle of humankind. This is known to geologists as "Pacifica" or "Sundaland," a large South Pacific land area that in ancient times was originally home to emigrants to India and Sumer to the west and to South and Central America to the east.

CENTRAL ASIA~TIBET

27. CENTRAL ASIA ~ TIBET

Central Asia in protohistoric times, before what Solon's Egyptian interlocutor referred to as the "Great Deluge of All," was a vast, fertile, temperate, well-watered area with huge numbers of large Pleistocene mammals such as the mammoth and the woolly rhinoceros. A high civilization existed in what is now the Gobi desert. This was destroyed in about 9600 BCE by an enormous flood, generated by either a massive passing Near Earth Object or by an actual NEO impact that destroyed the worldwide Atlantean civilization. This is evidenced by the islands virtually made up of the bones of countless millions of Pleistocene creatures that lie today to the north of Siberia and Alaska, washed up and deposited there by a flood coming from the south, of inconceivable size and power, that brought the Pleistocene Epoch to a sudden end.

The few survivors of this Gobi civilization, the unlettered people of the high mountains, slowly re-established themselves on the high plateaux of Tibet and Central Asia. Their resources were few and the climate, no longer temperate, was harsh and extreme. From them are descended the waves of savage warrior tribes who for centuries burned, slaughtered, raped and pillaged throughout an area from Europe in the west to China in the east. Attila the Hun (406–453 CE) was called "The Scourge of God" by mediaeval writers because of the widespread havoc wrought by his armies in Europe. Centuries later, he was followed by other invaders like the Golden Horde of Genghis Khan (1162–1227 CE), self-styled "King of the World," who burned and slaughtered from Europe to Beijing in establishing the First Mongol Empire, and by Tamerlane (1335–1405 CE), founder of the Second Mongol Empire, who destroyed the highly civilized Saracen Caliphate in Baghdad, conquered most of Persia, India and the Caucasus and was about to attack China when he died. His great grandson, Babur (1483–1530 CE), founded the Mogul (Mongol) Empire in Afghanistan and India.

The early Tibetans were also a warlike race whose empire once extended deep into China but who, under the gentle influence of Buddhism, were the very first nation voluntarily to renounce the use of arms and to establish a civilization based wholly on a religion dedicated to pacifism, that preached a doctrine of universal compassion.

The Tibetan region, in particular, has for many centuries been associated with the individual striving after spiritual advancement. The indigenous Bön religion was followed by the lofty teachings of Mahayana Buddhism, which absorbed the Bön Tantricism, derived originally from India, in its Tibetan form.

In more recent times, the Chinese invasion and occupation resulted in the more or less violent deaths of hundreds of thousands of innocent people. All of these events left their traces in the psyches of those involved, conquerors as well as those who were conquered. Your apparent incarnation or incarnations into these lost times will have left a deep, hence more readily accessible, mark on the psyche.

28. CENTRAL AMERICA

The Maya and the Aztecs are components of a complex of Central American cultures that, in the main, originated as colonies of Atlantis. Another very early tribal grouping, the mysterious Olmecs, was derived from streams of immigrants from, among others, Africa, India and China and included even people of Semitic origin, as is quite clear from Meso-American statuary and monuments. Of unknown origin are the Acámbaro figures of Mexico, dating back thousands of years and depicting recognizable prehistoric reptiles, supposedly destroyed by a NEO strike in Yucatan some sixty-five million years ago.

CENTRAL AMERICA

These cultures also describe the early civilizing influence of a tall, white, bearded teacher, whom they variously called Quetzalcoatl, Gucumatz and Kukulcan.

Quetzalcoatl is said to have arrived at the end of a long period of darkness that followed a cata-strophic Deluge. This cataclysm destroyed the advanced civiliza-tions of what was called the Fourth "Sun," or Fourth Age, of the world. He is said to have arrived by the sea and departed by the sea. He first appeared publicly in Mexico at Teotihuacan, "The place where men became gods." Like Viracocha/Kon Tiki in South America, Quetzalcoatl/Gucumatz/Kukulcan brought the benefits of civilization to a people that had been reduced to barbarism by a catastrophic event that involved the destruction of their ancestral homeland in the eastern ocean, that they called Atlan or Aztlan, from which only a few had managed to escape by sea, as depicted in the Mayan codices. It is likely that Viracocha, who also appeared from the sea, among the pre-Incas of South America, and Quetzalcoatl refer to the same man or group of men. Over the centuries, there has been much trans-oceanic contact between this area and the cultures of India, Indonesia, Southeast Asia, Japan, Korea and China, as is clearly shown by statuary and various monuments.

Hundreds of thousands of human beings were sacrificed to the gods in Meso-American cultures that were fearful of a recurrence of the Great Deluge that had destroyed their ancestors, leaving only a few survivors. They hoped thereby to forestall another such cataclysm.

Your vicarious Central American experience may have been peaceful or very traumatic indeed. It is the traumatic experiences that are most likely to have left their traces in the psyche.

29

SOUTH AMERICA

29. SOUTH AMERICA

Protohistoric South America is covered with ancient ruins, many of which date back fifty thousand years and more. This is one of the world's most mysterious and least researched regions. According to some South American archaeologists, recognizably modern human beings lived in South America as early as 300,000 BCE. The famous ICA stones of

Peru actually depict anatomically modern humans interacting with dinosaurs and performing heart and brain surgery. The huge rock carvings on the Marcahuasi Plateau, some of them depicting Pleistocene mammals, are completely mystifying to conventional anthropology. South America and southwestern North America were settled over many thousands of years by emigrants from "Mu"/"Lemuria"/Pacifica/Sundaland, in several waves throughout protohistoric times. The cataclysms that destroyed their Pacific homeland were associated with the tectonic forces that raised the Andes mountains.

This card symbolizes the great civilization that arose following the cataclysms that finally destroyed the Pacific Ocean culture. This new civilization was based at Tiahuanaco (Tiwanaku), near Lake Titicaca in the highlands of present-day Bolivia. Although now at an altitude of 12,500 feet above sea level, Tiahuanaco was a seaport, twelve to fifteen thousand years ago, as is evidenced by the existence of fossilized seashells and modified marine fauna in Lake Titicaca, on the shore of which the city was once located but which is now twelve miles distant and one hundred feet lower in altitude. The remains of an incredibly ancient civilization have also been discovered at the bottom of Lake Titicaca.

Some time after the last Great Deluge had flooded the world, plunged it into darkness, and destroyed the earlier civilization, Viracocha, known also as Kon Tiki, a tall, blue-eyed, bearded white man, brought knowledge that had been lost to the people, now reduced once again to barbarism. He and his companions conveyed to them the elements of medicine, metallurgy, farming, animal husbandry and an understanding of the principles of architecture and engineering. These early people then went on to build the vast network of roads and the impressive stone works that were later attributed to their remote descendants the Incas, who had simply inherited them and who preserved the early history of their forerunners in the form of myths and legends.

Viracocha/Kon Tiki is said to have both arrived and left South America by sea. It is likely that he subsequently appeared in Central America as Quetzalcoatl/Gucumatz/Kukulcan.

30

INDIGENOUS TRIBAL

30. INDIGENOUS TRIBAL

Thirty thousand years ago, tribal shamans were being depicted on the walls of Neolithic caves. In all human societies, before and since, there have been individuals who have been closer to Nature than their fellows. Such as they developed great psychic power through their close and continued attunement with the Source of all life. They were looked to for spiritual guidance and prophecy. They were also the medicine men and women of the tribe. Close to the forces of Nature, the indigenous culture was a deeply connected community, attuned to the cyclical nature of life. Many retained the memory of a great, fiery snake in the heavens that caused a black-as-night sky for days, associated with a devastating flood. Value was placed on oral traditions and the wisdom to be gained through shamanic journeys to other realms, which consequently benefited the entire society.

Many tribal societies have been forcibly torn from their spiritual moorings and callously destroyed by "civilized" white Europeans who deliberately burned, as "works of the Devil," entire libraries of the Maya and other Native American cultures. The "winning of the West" was a tragic *loss* for displaced tribes that had lived and prospered there since the earliest antediluvian times.

Examples of cultural chauvinism include the virtual destruction by white Europeans of the aboriginal Australians, who had adapted perfectly to life in a harsh land for sixty thousand years. The harmless, artistic and spiritual little Bushmen in southern Africa were actually hunted on horseback and slaughtered for "sport." Efforts by the European powers to enslave and to exploit the "natives" usually succeeded in wrenching them from their own tried and true traditions. The work of destruction continues today in the Amazon and elsewhere, where certain Christian missionaries actually deem it to be their holy duty literally to kill the native shaman.

Your selection of this card suggests incarnation of a projected personality into one or more of these myriad tribal cultures that have suffered so much unsought and unwelcome attention from foreign invaders. Your association with an indigenous tribal culture, as either perpetrator or victim of such crimes, was likely very traumatic, hence capable of leaving a strong trace in the psyche.

31. ALIEN

The universe is alive, conscious and mental. Within that universal consciousness there has arisen a virtually infinite number and variety of apparent life forms, in any or all of which your projected personality may have vicariously experienced incarnation.

Your choice of this card suggests many meanings. Not all of them necessarily have to do with reincarnation as such. On the one hand, the memories it triggers may be valid recollections of a past or indeed of a future apparent embodiment. On the other hand, it may awaken experiences you appear to have undergone in your current incarnation that you have forgotten because your recall of them has been intentionally blocked by "screen memories," imposed either by extraterrestrial or other-dimensional aliens, or by yourself out of fear or reluctance to accept the actuality of the experience.

Above all, take comfort in knowing that you have nothing to fear from this or from any other recollection that comes to you in the course of using these cards. The objective of your research is to gain access to psychic impressions that are normally not open to your present, everyday egoic personality. As you gain experience in acquiring such access, you will increasingly view these glimpses with greater and greater objectivity, as if they had happened to someone else — as indeed they did!

The One that you really *are* forever stands above and beyond all episodes that appear to be experienced by your various emanated, incarnate, ephemeral personalities. The realization of this supreme *fact* is the ultimate purpose of these adventures in self-directed psychical research.

◇ **Environment Cards — Introduction**

Every incarnation is framed by an environment, a scene against the background of which that particular life's myriad events appear to unfold. There are nine of these cards, some of which may resonate deeply within you.

A particular environment may play an integral role in a life's apparent experiences as shaped by the diverse landscapes of the planet, each with its own beauties and hardships. Such experiences, molded by the often sharp and relentless forces of nature, may provide insights into the seeming vulnerability and physical mortality of a human being. Equally, an individual may gain access to mystical and spiritual states of intense emotional bliss and intellectual understanding through a deeply felt connection to the magnificent, powerful energies of the Planet Earth. Through such experiences, one may acquire an awareness of one's true nature and its relationship of identity to Universal Consciousness.

It is most useful to think about the selected environment card in the context of cards of other categories that have been drawn at the same time. It might be thought that cards of different categories which, to outer appearances, have been randomly selected, would have no relationship to each other. It has been found, however, that they often do appear synchronistically to have been subconsciously chosen to appear together. You are expected to seek within yourself for the connections that your superconscious, Higher Self is trying in this way to display to you.

32. DESERT

32

DESERT

This card depicts a bleak, inhospitable, but visually grand environment. It may usually be taken to suggest a life of deprivation and actual hardship, during which the struggle for sheer survival may have been hard and pitiless — a physically difficult life bereft of luxuries and characterized by chronic shortages of vital necessities such as food and water.

Such deprived, desert environments naturally encourage the emergence of warlike societies. To survive, your emanated personality may have been forced to commit or to suffer many actions that, from a more peaceful and tranquil perspective, may appear to be unfortunate or even cruel and heartless.

As a compensation, however, in your projected personality, you were given the opportunity to rise above your harsh surroundings and to gain a genuine spiritual benefit through an inner triumph of the so-called "individual soul" over outer adversity.

Your contemplation of the awesome vistas and vast silence of the desert contributed to your mastery of your lower self, or egoic mind. Difficult as this incarnation may have appeared to be in the purely physical sense, it must be counted a blessing.

FOREST

33. FOREST

Many of your apparent projections into incarnation have been passed in a forest environment. In the earlier periods of physical evolution, as a true forest creature, you actually experienced life in the trees, subsisting primarily on fruits, nuts, seeds and insects. In the course of time, you also experienced so-called lives as a hunter or a gatherer, charged with the responsibility of finding food for yourself and your family.

During such embodiments your emanated personality may have been far closer to nature than you find yourself to be in your present incarnation. Forests are often associated in folklore as home to the magical kingdoms of elves, fairies and nature spirits. You may have acquired a sense of wonder, respect and deep connectedness to wooded glens from encounters with such energies in other apparent incarnations.

If you look upon a forested environment with nostalgia, yearning still for the peace that may be found when alone in grove or glade, you may find it to be helpful to focus your attention on feelings of this kind. In this way you may evoke the many resonances that can arise from concentration on this woodland environment.

It is recommended that, again and again, you allow your consciousness to blend into the silence to be found in the forest.

34. MOUNTAIN

Many an incarnation has been apparently passed in a mountainous environment.

From Arunachala in the south to the majestic Himalayas in the north of India and in Tibet, as well as elsewhere in the world, people in search of peace and wisdom have been drawn to the high places.

Accordingly, you may easily resonate with this card in many ways. You will note, however, that the majestic mountain scenery is viewed by a lone figure, seated in a cave. This is the "Cave of Contemplation." The person who is gazing peacefully at the distant mountains is indicative of a self-imposed life of physical denial, during which normal creature comforts and the society of family and friends were deliberately forsaken, if only temporarily, in the pursuit of an intended spiritual path — a search within for the One over the egoic self.

When you draw and study this card, try to still all thoughts and to remain in a state of unbroken conscious awareness, knowing that you forever carry the "Cave of Contemplation" in your heart.

35

FIELDS

35. FIELDS

This card suggests a more or less placid life passed in a rural setting. Your projected personality may have been involved in the raising of livestock and in the growing of various kinds of produce, vegetables, fruits and cereals.

Although generally quiet and relatively uneventful, in some periods the agricultural life could be very precarious and difficult. Crop failure can lead to widespread famine. Your welfare and that of your family depended completely on adequate rainfall and other generally benign weather conditions. Agriculturists made possible the rise of modern civilization, but the greater part of the benefits of such prosperity, then as now, have only rarely trickled down to their level. Life in such conditions can be poor and harsh, with success both limited and uncertain. Wars and wholesale theft by the powerful may also have made an impact.

Yet such is the resilience and adaptability of humankind, that they were able to survive and even to flourish, passing on their acquired skills and seeds to their descendants.

36. RIVERINE

Given the vital need for fresh water, human beings have always settled along the banks of rivers and on the shores of lakes. The growth of cultures has taken place along such great rivers as the Nile, Tigris, Euphrates, Ganges, Indus, Brahmaputra, Mekong, Yang-tse, Amazon, Mississippi, St. Lawrence, Seine, Rhine, Hudson, Tiber, Thames, Congo, etc. The need for ready access to water, however, rendered these cultures especially

36

RIVERINE

vulnerable to destruction by periodic, cataclysmic floods, which have totally destroyed entire civilizations in the past.

Many projected lives have been passed in a lake setting. The lakeside community, usually a village largely supported by a freshwater fishery, was very common in the past as a way of life in early Europe and America and down to the present time in large parts of Asia. This card depicts such a life in a fishing village erected on stilts as in primitive middle Europe or as in a more or less modern kampong in southeast Asia.

Life in such a setting is normally based on cooperation with others. In some areas it also has its dangers. Even today in some places, crocodiles take many who believe themselves to be safe from such attack.

If this card resonates strongly with you, it is highly likely that you are experiencing an echo of an apparent embodiment in such an environment in the past.

37. TOWN

Many incarnations have been vicariously experienced by you through your various emanated personas in a town, village or hamlet environment, in both peaceful and troubled times.

You may have known life as a personage of some local consequence or, more commonly, as a virtually unknown individual. This card depicts a less-isolated life in this setting. Here one enjoys the society of one's fellows in normally, but not always, peaceful surroundings.

In the absence of war or civil disturbance, life in such an environment was tranquil and relatively unchallenging. In times of war or revolution, however, the town-dweller or rustic villager has all too often been the victim of the lusts and greed of the powerful. Such experiences may have been highly traumatic and will likely have left their scars on the psyche. Otherwise, your psychic impressions are more likely to involve the memory of

particular individuals, characters that you may be able to recognize in your current life situation.

38. CITY

Throughout human history people have gathered in cities. This history extends back far beyond Rome, Alexandria, Athens, Eridu or Atlantis. Tiwanaku's history may have extended back as far as fifteen thousand years. Remote and romantic as those urban complexes may appear when viewed from today, they suffered from the same drawbacks as does any really large

38

CITY

conglomeration of people in one location, including modern cities. Crowded, unhygienic conditions set the stage for epidemics such as the plagues that wiped out a huge percentage of Europeans in the late Middle Ages.

Countless millions of innocent city-dwellers have been massacred over the centuries, from Genghis Khan's rape of Beijing and Tamerlane's "mountain of skulls" in Baghdad to the World War Two "Blitz" of London, the "carpet-bombings" of German cities and the nuclear incineration of Hiroshima and Nagasaki.

In all such clustered masses of humanity there are also vast disparities of prosperity among the people. Inequalities of this kind can generate resonances of the harshness of the conditions, the "dark, satanic mills" in which an incarnation may have been passed.

The reverse may also be experienced. A city inhabitant of comfortable material means may feel stimulated and energized by the diverse opportunities presented by a thick concentration of many types of people and all that this entails.

Indeed, a city environment is a stage for all of the contrasting variables of incarnate experience. As such, this card may evoke numerous resonances for you to contemplate.

39. MARINE

39

MARINE

Contrary to modern opinion generally, humankind have for countless centuries crossed and re-crossed the oceans of the world. There is unimpeachable evidence in the form of ancient maps, of the existence of a world-wide, high maritime civilization during the last (Wisconsin) Ice Age, that was totally destroyed by the same cataclysm that simultaneously brought the Ice Age to an end in about 9600 BCE. That antediluvian civilization was only the last of a long series of such civilizations that had been similarly terminated by catastrophic events untold ages ago.

Early humans, like the more recent Polynesians, were seafaring people, to whom oceans are not a barrier, but a highway. Your selection of this card suggests that one or more of your projected incarnate personalities was much involved with the sea. You may wish to allow your mind to dwell on this, letting your imagination run free.

The variety of sea-going vessels, ancient and modern, may suggest to you a life or lives as a sailor, fisher, navigator, sea captain or even a pirate or a galley slave. Record all details of any evoked impressions in your journal.

As always, however, it would be wise to leave the *final* interpretation of this card until you ascertain how it fits in with the experiences and life characteristics that are suggested by other cards.

40

SEASHORE

40. SEASHORE

In very ancient times, perhaps even before *homo* became *sapiens,* humans went through an extended period, in the course of which they underwent physical evolution as a semi-aquatic species. These early primate ancestors were forced by the need to forage, as well as to escape from large, savage predators, to find both easily obtainable food and personal safety in the shallows of the sea. Other mammals, like the whales, porpoises and dugongs, are descended from terrestrial animals that returned permanently to the oceans. Still others, like the sea otters, seals, walruses, polar bears and sea lions, spend much of their lives in the sea but continue to breed on land, where they pass a large part of their time.

To a somewhat lesser extent, humans, the only "diving primates" only partly returned to the sea. This was, however, for a long enough period, between one and two million years, probably during the Miocene Epoch (23.8 to 5.3 million years ago) or even earlier.

Over time, they came physically to be partially adapted to this environment, losing much of their body hair, and developing webbed fingers and toes, a subcutaneous fat layer, tear glands, a descended larynx and enlarged breasts. This early survival mode lasted until such time as it was safe to emerge from the shallows completely for an essentially permanent life on land, unlike other former land mammals that had migrated permanently back to the oceans.

Even today people enjoy restful and refreshing vacations at the seaside and swimming at beaches, prompted by a folk memory derived from forebears, who for countless millennia passed much of their time in the shallows.

Drawing this card does not necessarily suggest an incarnation in that most remote period of human evolution. It may well contain hints of embodiments of a much more recent time. Many have been drawn to the seashore throughout the ages. Still, the dangers faced by our very early physical progenitors were very real, such as that encountered in connection with sharks, saltwater crocodiles, and the invariably deadly poisonous sea snakes. Such experiences have left their effects on your psyche at a deep level.

+ THEME CARDS — INTRODUCTION

These eleven cards are intended to summarize any one apparent incarnation — to highlight both the main trends of and the lessons to be learned from the events vicariously experienced in the course of a particular apparent embodiment.

These cards reflect the individual character displayed by your projected personality, which is different and distinct for each incarnation, during that lifetime.

There are many lessons to be learned here. Certain patterns appear in diverse apparent incarnations, which provide opportunities to revisit a particular theme or life lesson in its many guises.

Perhaps the most important of these is that you come to understand the passing, ephemeral nature of the projected personality, as distinguished from your higher individuality, forever at the center of the wheel of the Higher Self, or Atman.

41. ABUNDANCE ~ PENURY

Rich or poor, all superficial personalities share the same end. Both extremes of physical prosperity are represented by this card. A life of plentiful material wealth and one of great need for the basics of survival may be found in one incarnation immediately after the other extreme in the previous apparent embodiment. Thus an appropriate balance is struck to help you to advance in understanding the cyclical, dreamlike nature of all worldly experience.

More important than the wealth of resources, or the lack of them, then at your projected personality's command, however, is how it chose to use them. If one's fate is such as to have had the burden of wealth thrust upon one, it should be considered as a trust, to be dispensed wisely in the greater interest of all. Great wealth thus represents a correspondingly great opportunity and responsibility. One lesson to be learned is that abundance should

41

ABUNDANCE~PENURY

never be either a source of pride or sought for its own sake. Such an objective on the personality's part would be unworthy of you. Jesus, Ramakrishna and the Maharishi Ramana had no need for affluence, and the Buddha, although born to wealth, renounced it. These are far more worthy role models than symbols of great material wealth like Croesus, Rockefeller or Rothschild.

The experience of penury need never be sought, but should always be welcome if that is what comes. A life of physical deprivation may provide many opportunities for a deeper understanding of the fleeting nature of existence. Lessons to be learned include patience, humility and inner courage in the face of outer adversity.

GROWTH

42. GROWTH

Your selection of this beautiful card indicates a lifetime characterized by steady spiritual growth — an advance through the incarnations, toward knowing who you really are through achieving an ever greater insight into the reality of universal consciousness.

The symbol of the chambered nautilus shell inspired Oliver Wendell Holmes (1809 –1894) to write:

Year after year beheld the silent toil
That spread his lustrous coil;
Still, as the spiral grew,
He left the past year's dwelling for the new,
Stole with soft step its shining archway through,
Built up its idle door,
Stretched in his last-found home, and knew the old no more.

Thanks for the heavenly message brought by thee
Child of the wandering sea,

Cast from her lap, forlorn!
From thy dead lips a clearer note is born
Than ever Triton blew from wreathéd horn!
While on my ear it rings,
Through the deep caves of thought I hear a voice that sings:

Build thee more stately mansions, O my soul
As the swift seasons roll!
Leave thy low-vaulted past!
Let each new temple, nobler than the last,
Shut thee from heaven with a dome more vast,
Till thou at length art free,
Leaving thine outworn shell by life's unresting sea!

You will do well to meditate on these words and to absorb to the full the message they contain.

Similarly, the symbol of the butterfly emerging from the no-longer-needed cocoon also denotes a period of actual transformation to a higher spiritual perspective.

43. JUSTICE ~ INJUSTICE

Many, indeed virtually all, people have been treated in ways that they consider to be unjust at various times in their present as well as in their former apparent lifetimes. If a sense of injustice

43

JUSTICE~INJUSTICE

resonates with you on drawing this card, it may well be an indication that one or more of your projected incarnate personalities underwent such an experience or, on the contrary, was itself responsible for inflicting it on others.

This carries with it a warning that you must learn to accept whatever apparent evil may have been vicariously visited upon you, in confidence that the law of Karma will ensure that it will all balance out in the end. You should always accept, without reserve, what *is*. Put away any idea of victimhood, which can only stand in the way of enlightenment. You must learn to forgive and to forget, however terrible the harm, physical or psychical, that may have been apparently suffered by your projected personality. Then, having absorbed whatever lesson it had to teach you, the time has come simply to let it go.

If it is your projected personality that has appeared to inflict injustice on another or others, the same applies. In the knowledge that whatever is, *is* in the Eternal Now, let it go. Such total *acceptance* will set you free.

44. STABILITY ~ INSTABILITY

On the one hand, the Great (Khufu) Pyramid has stood for thousands of years and will stand for many more. For you, it represents the very essence of patience, quiet strength and stability. If, on the other hand, the collapsing tower resonates with you, rather than the pyramid, the projected personality in that particular lifetime may have appeared to experience, for long periods of time, strong feelings derived from episodes of great uncertainty and insecurity. At its most severe, actual physical or emotional breakdown may have been experienced by that apparent individual.

If this should be so, you may wish to look within to try to identify the cause of such intuitions so as to be able to confront them direct and thereby to cauterize any negative emotions or phobias that may originate from that time.

In any event, make sure that you write them up in as great detail as possible in your journal. Recording them in that way is in itself extremely salutary.

STABILITY ~ INSTABILITY

45. LOVE ~ INDIFFERENCE

Your selection of this card suggests a vicariously experienced lifetime dominated by emotion. This could involve either love, in a wonderfully warm, harmonious physical and spiritual relationship with another or others, or eventual estrangement and the consequent loneliness and despair that can arise at the end of a love that has run its course. This may result in a lack of affection leading to complete indifference that, in the extreme, may even have degenerated into hatred.

Highly emotional episodes of this kind leave deep scars in the psyche of the individual personality that you appear to have projected into that particular incarnation. If this card resonates strongly with you, you may wish to look around you in your current apparent incarnational environment, to try to identify others among your present-day family and acquaintances, with whom your other personal projection was so closely involved.

The same "souls" tend to meet each other over and over until all such disharmonies are resolved.

46. POWER

The symbol of the thunderbolt or lightning strike indicates an emanated apparent lifetime characterized by the possession and exercise of power, over oneself and/or over others. This power may have been physical, mental, psychic or spiritual.

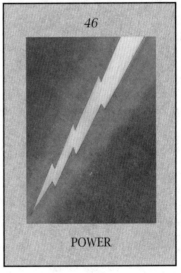

You must know, however, that with power comes responsibility. The incarnate personality's greatest problem was, and remains, the need to exercise firm control over itself and not to abuse the weak and the defenseless. Much adverse Karma can result from these unequal situations, but all is forgiven in the end. There is no Purgatory or Hell — just another chance to do better this time.

POWER

47. CREATIVITY ~ DESTRUCTIVENESS

Each incarnated personality has elements of both of these characteristics to some extent.

Creativity may be expressed in so many ways. On this card, the potter at the wheel is making a beautiful vase to be given to

47

CREATIVITY~
DESTRUCTIVENESS

others. Depending upon how it resonates with you, this card suggests a lifetime in which your projected personality may have lived creatively, always seeking out new ideas, embarking on new enterprises, gladly cooperating with others, generally inspired by a spirit of optimism, cheerful even in the face of adversity.

On the contrary, the smashed pots suggest a negative approach to life, constant complaint, frustration and disapproval of the actions and thoughts of others. Always looking back to the past, not living in the present or looking forward to the future. The futility of such an ego-dominated outlook should now be clear to you.

48. FREEDOM ~ SERVITUDE

Many apparent incarnations have been experienced in which your projected personality may have been in a position of servitude, more or less subject to the will of others. You may even have known actual slavery, either as slave or as master/mistress.

There is no shame in such a situation or indeed in any vicariously experienced incarnation. If your projected personality were the slave-owner, it is not to be blamed for the societal imperative that placed it in that role any more than if it were the slave.

In this, as in all such situations, it is necessary only that we try to treat one another with kindness and consideration. This is yet another case in which, if you look about you, it may be

48

FREEDOM~SERVITUDE

possible to identify a person in your present apparent lifetime with whom you shared such a relationship in the past. Do not be surprised if you find that the roles have been reversed!

49. GREED ~ GENEROSITY

On drawing this card, you may be intuitively aware of the lessons learned in an apparent lifetime characterized by an egoistic, selfish urge to acquire and to hoard or, on the contrary, by an incarnation during which your projected personality was always ready, however poor you may have been, charitably to extend a compassionate, helping hand to others.

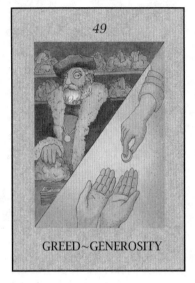

49

GREED~GENEROSITY

Much experience has probably taught you that it is almost always the poor who are generous to the poor and that those who have much tend frequently to hoard selfishly what they have, and to want more. Viewed in this way, depending upon the character of the experiencer, it is possible to be cursed with wealth and blessed with poverty. There are many valuable lessons for both rich and poor to be learned in such an incarnation.

50. BETRAYAL

Your choice of this card suggests the lifetime of a projected personality that was characterized by an act or acts of betrayal, either as perpetrator or as victim. Unfortunately, such is the ego-dominated human nature that most lives have seemed to be blighted by acts involving deception or treachery of one sort or another.

Such acts, inspired by fear of imagined "others," are typical of the self-isolated, egoic mind's felt need for security. In its feverish search for ways to support its false belief in the independence, hence the supreme importance of itself, the egoic mind is capable of heinous acts of unspeakable cruelty as viewed from the level of the projected personality.

Although such acts may appear to leave an indelible trace on the psyche, you will realize that, ultimately, there is no "betrayer" just as there is no "betrayed." True insight perceives that, in essence, All is One.

Whatever your projected personality may have *appeared* to do to "another," it was, ironically, doing only to itself.

50

BETRAYAL

51. FEAR

This card depicts a reflection in a hand-held mirror of one's innermost fears and demons. Mistakenly projected outward without understanding the source in our egoic mind, this reflection mirrors our misperception of who we really are. On a simpler level of interpretation, this card may represent a phobia or deeply held seemingly irrational fear, stemming from a traumatic episode in another apparent embodiment.

In all *apparent* incarnations, including the present one, for the incarnate personality there is an ever-present, if unrecognized

51

FEAR

undercurrent of fear. Believing itself to have been created in time, each separate incarnate personality consequently fears its own destruction. At the highest level, you, the *actual* experiencer, *know* that the events and the projected personality are *ultimately* illusory and that whatever appears at one moment in time *must,* inevitably, disappear at another moment in time. The projected personality itself normally fails to perceive this, but is still somehow aware of its *essential* immortality.

The incompatibility of this awareness with the hypnotically held but false belief in the permanent reality of the incarnate personality, or egoic mind, has serious consequences. The personality does not know that, although *essentially* immortal, it is but one of a veritable galaxy of simultaneously existent personalities that you appear to have projected into serial incarnation. Consequently, it has confused its false belief in the permanent reality of its ego with its intuitive knowledge of its essential immortality. Thereafter, it erroneously believes in the immortality of the temporary personal ego, which it calls its "immortal soul." The projected ego's efforts are then directed to preserving itself, inspired by a fear of the death of the egoic mind, or "soul." Such efforts are bound to fail.

True immortality is not an indefinite perpetuation of the current personality. It is, on the contrary, an *escape from the bonds* of personality into the true nirvanic freedom of supreme Self-awareness, or "God"-consciousness.

"One who knows for certain that this universe is but an illusion and a nothing, becomes desireless and Pure Intelligence, and finds peace as if nothing exists."

Astavakra Samhita XV–17

∞ TERMINATION CARDS — INTRODUCTION

These ten cards are designed to trigger your memories of the circumstances in which a projected personality came to the end of an apparent incarnation. Know that, through these emanations, you experience them all, not once but many times, in the long course of your personal history, past and future. At one time, it was believed that physical evolution proceeded at a slow but steady pace, a theory known as *uniformitarianism*. In this view, the passage of immensely long periods of time is sufficient to explain all changes. Catastrophes either never happen or need not be allowed for.

Nevertheless, it is a fact that organic life on Earth has been all but totally destroyed on at least five occasions in the planet's prehistory. There is reason to believe that the causes of such vast destruction, as with the interstadial event that effectively wiped out the dinosaurs and ended the Mesozoic Era, some sixty-five million years ago, or the terrible event that ended the Pleistocene Epoch, were collisions with the Earth by a Near Earth Object such as a comet or an asteroid, or by the near-passage of a massive body that generated immense tidal surges.

History is full of catastrophic events, recorded and unrecorded, as well as countless wars, raids for plunder, rapes and murders. For long periods, incarnate human life was indeed largely "nasty, brutish and short." Famines and plagues, as well as savage predators, like bears, wolves, lions, crocodiles and sharks, have carried off countless people. For century after century, it was only relatively rarely that one died in peace, carefree and surrounded by one's loved ones. The *Termination* cards reflect these various outcomes.

Studying these cards from the impersonal view of an uninvolved observer, one comes gradually to perceive the ephemerality of apparent existence in a physical body. One learns that one is indeed far, far more than the physical body and more even than any of one's projected superficial personalities; that death is only a change of one incarnational scene to another on the stage of beginningless and endless, timeless consciousness.

52. PEACEFUL

Whatever the circumstances or general life situation of any of your projected incarnations may have been, you have often vicariously experienced the peace of a transition surrounded by loving friends and family. Your selection of this card suggests a tranquil ending to what may or may not have been a tumultuous incarnation as known to your projected personality.

52

PEACEFUL

Each transition is an opportunity to merge into the One Universal Consciousness that is your real Self. On each occasion of this kind, you have known, however briefly, the truth of these words of Prospero from the Tempest, written by that great sage known to posterity only by his *nom de plume,* William Shakespeare:

Our revels now are ended. These our actors,
As I foretold you, were all spirits, and
Are melted into air, into thin air.
And like the baseless fabric of this vision
The cloud-capped towers, the gorgeous palaces,
The solemn temples, the great globe itself,
Yea, all which it inherit, shall dissolve,
And like this insubstantial pageant faded
Leave not a rack behind. We are such stuff
As dreams are made on; and our little life
Is rounded with a sleep . . .

53. WATER

Countless deaths are caused by water. Rivers burst their banks, causing widespread flooding, people fall into pools or lakes, are drowned by tsunamis generated by submarine earthquakes, or are carried out to sea by high tides or undetected rip currents.

Such transitions must be considered as virtually normal. Life on Earth, however, has been all but totally destroyed on at least five occasions in the planet's pre-history, such as the event, sixty-five million years ago, that effectively wiped out the dinosaurs and ended the Mesozoic Era. These were caused by collisions of the Earth with a Near Earth Object such as a comet or an asteroid. Yet another, more recent such event,

WATER

involved either the impact of such an object in the Atlantic Ocean or the near passage of a massive body in about 9600 BCE, that both generated huge tsunamis and brought the last Ice Age to a sudden end. While there have been many such events that have been lost to memory, this one gave rise to what, thanks to Plato, has gone down in history as what the Egyptian priest described to Solon as the Great Deluge of All. This Deluge is known to virtually all peoples across the world and has been incorporated into their myths and legends, as in the Bible, the Epic of Gilgamesh, the Mayan Codices, the Floods of Deucalion and Ogyges, and countless others.

Quite aside from normal drownings, all people now incarnate have experienced this trauma in the past. Your selection of this one card, more than almost any other, is likely to trigger a far memory of your projected personality's presence at such a cataclysmic event. The picture of an approaching wall of water, hundreds of feet high, inevitably to result in the termination and violent transition of you and your loved ones, left an indelible impression that was seared into your consciousness at the deepest level. Helpless and in despair, you could only await the transition with as much courage as you could muster, resigned to the decree of Fate. You now know, however, that this experience, like all others, passed away and that you are now, as indeed you were even then, free from any lasting harm.

FIRE

54. FIRE

Early humans owed their survival to their ability to master and to utilize naturally occurring fire, as from lightning strikes, to warm themselves, to cook their food, and to drive away dangerous animals.

Yet, while a friend of humanity, fire can also be a very dangerous enemy if not treated with the greatest respect. Forest and prairie fires have taken countless lives as have fires inadvertently caused in homes from the earliest times.

Aside from deaths by accident, however, many thousands of people have been deliberately put to death by fire for having had the temerity not to meet the standards of behavior and belief laid down by the majority among whom they were so unfortunate as to reside. Inquisitions and witch-hunts have been instituted by the intolerant majority throughout the ages. Fire has often been the execution method of choice to do away with those who have transgressed the norms of their fellows.

Thousands of people have perished in fires as well as by nuclear radiation generated in the course of the bombing of cities in times of war and other offensive actions. Death by fire is extremely traumatic and highly likely to have left a very sharp and distinct impression on the individual psyche.

Your selection of this card may trigger a memory of an experience as either an innocent victim, a witness, or even as an instigator of such an incident. Whether punisher or punished, however, it must be regarded now as it was even then, as simply another temporary state of consciousness to be viewed with total detachment and thus to be transcended.

55. WAR

The primary activity of the human species appears to be tribal warfare. At least one hundred million humans were slaughtered in the course of wars in the twentieth century alone. Throughout history, from the earliest protohistoric and prehistoric periods, people have been killing people for what they believe to be gain.

55

WAR

Most people, the vast majority, are immured in a false belief that, as individuals, they are forever separate from and independent of both an "outside world" and the universal consciousness in which they live and move and have their Being.

In our ignorance, struggling as "individuals" constantly at war with each other, we seek to acquire and to accumulate material possessions at the expense of "others." We try to gain control over and to exploit them because we fail to perceive them as our very Self. This basic fault in perception is a spiritually blind condition that is induced in people by habitually viewing the world through the distorting lens of the personal ego — a fundamental failure of the reasoning process. Such disordered reason is properly called *insanity*. It comes as a rude shock to these people to learn that, to the extent that their egoistic actions are driven by this false belief, held with hypnotic force, *they are plainly and simply insane*. The consequences of this failure in perception are to be seen everywhere, in countless examples of "man's humanity to man." Not "inhumanity." What could be more typically human than aggressive wars, theft, pillage, rape and murder?

You have certainly vicariously experienced the worst horrors of warfare on many, many occasions throughout your reincarnational history. Such memories, if you have not deliberately blocked them out, should be more readily accessible to you than are most others. Their recollection can assist you to learn to *see through* the all-too-normal insanity of our species and the illusion of separateness generated by the personal ego. Perceive the inner light in all others and recognize them as your very Self. See *all* creatures, human and non-human, animate and inanimate, terrestrial or "alien," as One. There truly is no "other" in this or any world or universe.

56. SUICIDE

This card depicts a self-inflicted termination as the culmination of a set of circumstances that led its victim to consider continued physical existence in that apparent incarnation as no longer bearable. This is in no way to be condemned. From the individual incarnate personality's point of view, given his or her level of consciousness at the time, it was the right and only course of action; one that would not otherwise have been embarked upon.

There are lessons to be learned from this experience. One of the most important of these is that life does indeed go on. The ephemeral body can easily be destroyed but the underlying consciousness, the true Self, is immortal. There is no sin here. All is forgiven because one is understood and unconditionally loved, however dismal and unhappy the outer circumstances may have *appeared* to be.

The act of suicide does, however, affect others who are close to one, such as family and friends. Not only your own, but also their lives are changed by this experience, in terms of lessons learned and their own subsequent life experiences. You are likely to encounter many of the same individuals in the course of other apparent embodiments, including the current one.

It should be noted that suicide takes many forms, often not recognized as such, from seemingly heroic deaths in battle to over-indulgence in food, drink or drugs. All such self-destructive activities are suicidal in nature, as they are, consciously or unconsciously, intended to change the circumstances in which one finds oneself, including the outer personality manifest in that particular incarnation, with which one no longer wishes to identify oneself.

57. ATTACK

Although this card appears to suggest sudden deliberate termination at the hands of another human being, its meaning extends far beyond this, to include, as well, the violent termination of an incarnation caused by any other living creature.

57

ATTACK

One may have succumbed to an attack by a predator such as a shark or crocodile during a semi-aquatic period of evolution, a gigantic cave bear or sabre-tooth-ed cat, a dire wolf, a mammoth or, even earlier, a Tyrannosaurus Rex or Velociraptor. Death due to snake-bite is also not uncommon. Sea-snakes are invariably poison-ous and would have been a particular danger during a semi-aquatic apparent incarnation, as are many terrestrial species. The very common fear of snakes is often a phobia that is subconsciously induced by such a memory.

The attack category might also include death due to warfare, but there are reasons for treating war as a separate category of experience.

The sudden, usually shocking, end to an apparent incarnation through an act of violence may generate strong emotions that leave pronounced scars on the psyche. These feelings, when regarded with detachment and thereby released, can be a gateway to understanding more fully your true nature as infinite Cosmic Mind.

58

ACCIDENT

58. ACCIDENT

Although this card depicts a person falling to his or her death from a high place, it is intended to stand for any death by an accident involving the victim's violent collision with a concrete object. The episode may have been a collision with an automobile or chariot or any sort of traffic accident, an airplane crash, the collapse of a building, or even something as prosaic as a sports injury, one incurred during military or para-military training, or even an accidental fall off a ladder or down a flight of stairs.

Fatal injuries of this kind are primarily injuries to the cerebro-spinal system, especially to the head.

The death and transition of the projected personality can be very traumatic and sudden in those circumstances. Your selection of this card may suggest that one of your projected personalities has undergone such an experience to which you are now resonating. Sudden violent transitions of this kind can often result in phobias such as a fear of heights, that have been carried over into the current incarnation from an earlier apparent embodiment.

One should try to determine the cause of such fears so that, by facing them squarely and understanding their origin, one may eliminate them.

59. DISEASE

59

DISEASE

Termination by disease has always been a commonplace event throughout history. The card you have chosen suggests a termination in an epidemic such as the Black Plague that, starting from China in the year 1347 CE, more than decimated Europe in the Middle Ages. In the years 1348–50 CE it is variously estimated that this disease, probably bubonic plague, killed between one-quarter and one-third of the population of Europe. In an epidemic, vast numbers of individuals depart the physical rather suddenly. At the height of such an event, only the most courageous people ventured out of doors to attend to such unhappy and dangerous chores as the removal of the bodies of victims for incineration or burial.

Aside from epidemics, the poor state of hygiene could render fatal any penetrating wound, even little more than a scratch. Given the relatively poor level of medical knowledge throughout long stretches of humanity's vast early periods of earthly history, all currently incarnate humans have vicariously experienced any number of disease-caused terminations in the past. An example of a widespread modern phobia is that of a dread of dentists and doctors, which may be linked to deeply buried far memories of lingering, painful deaths of so many incarnates who suffered systemic poisoning by an infected tooth or a septic wound.

Your selection of this card may induce a memory of your apparent incarnation as a victim of disease or as one who did his or her best to relieve the situation, either by caring for the sick or by removing their bodies from the scene.

It is desirable that you spend much time in contemplating this card so as to determine its meaning for you. What was your purpose in undergoing that experience? What did you learn from it?

In the end, you will perceive that all such experiences, although they certainly may be said to *exist*, are ultimately unreal.

60. CATASTROPHE

Aside from the Great Deluge of about 9600 BCE, on at least five occasions this planet has been struck by a Near Earth Object (NEO) of such magnitude as to all but destroy the life that had evolved on it up to that time. These major events happened 440 million, 365 million, 250 million, 210 million and 65 million years BP. There is also evidence of more than 150 such impacts, the scars of which, owing to the Earth's climate, have been weathered beyond easy recognition.

In addition to the ever-present danger posed by NEOs, this is a most unstable planet. Aside from frequent relatively small strikes by objects from the heavens, such as the 1908 CE Tunguska Event in Siberia, the Earth's crust is in constant tectonic movement. Earthquakes are always occurring, some of them major, that often wreak much havoc in built-up areas. In

CATASTROPHE

certain parts of the world, especially along the so-called Ring of Fire around the Pacific Ocean, through the Mediterranean, in the Caribbean area, in South Asia and in China, devastating earthquakes and volcanic eruptions have killed countless millions of people, who are often trapped inside buildings, unable to escape. In addition to deaths by the direct impact of falling debris, many die by suffocation before they can be rescued.

Your selection of this card suggests that one or probably many more of your projected individual personalities underwent a very traumatic experience of this kind. It is possible that, as a consequence, in your present apparent incarnation you suffer from a fear of enclosed spaces. If so, and you succeed in recalling the origin of this claustrophobia in precise detail, you will almost certainly be able either to reduce its influence on your current personality or to eliminate it entirely.

However that may be, it is helpful to understand that whatever happened to your secondary, projected personality during any particular incarnation or incarnations not only cannot hurt you now, but also could not hurt the real you even then, no matter how frightening or shocking the experience may have appeared to be at that time.

STARVATION

61. STARVATION

Even today, deaths by outright starvation, not including those indirectly caused by malnutrition, number in the millions every year. From the earliest times, the human situation has been one of feast or famine, the latter far more common than the former. Famine has been so common in the unwritten history of humanity that no one who is apparently incarnate today has not known it vicariously in other incarnations. There are no exceptions to this. Everyone has had this experience, not once but any number of times.

There have frequently been periods when crop failure due to lack of seasonal rains has led to widespread famine and multiple deaths by starvation. Moreover, in times of war, food production is often disrupted. Food supplies are commandeered by armies. There is widespread killing of unfortunate populations, defenseless and at the mercy of invading hordes. Agricultural workers are killed or conscripted, leaving few to tend the fields, which may have been destroyed in any case. Following mass destruction in the wake of conquering armies, survivors of the slaughter are left to starve.

You may also have had the experience of being lost in the wilderness, exhausted and unable to go on. You were incapable of surviving physically and died of starvation and exposure, alone in the wild.

Your selection of this card suggests an incarnation in which the personality that you then projected may have known this experience in a most direct, personal way. If so, this card will resonate with you sooner or later. You now know, of course, that however traumatic the actual experience may have appeared to be at that time, the real you, the higher individuality, looking on quite impersonally, was not affected in the least. As your center of consciousness shifted to the level of the higher individuality, the Overself or Atman, you realized for yourself the ultimate unreality of the scene and that the life, as you thought of it then, was very much like a dream — as indeed is your current incarnation clearly seen to be if viewed from the same impersonal level.

$\mathcal{S}$*even* . . . THE SECRET

The questions posed in the first paragraph of Chapter One of this book must now be addressed. What is it that incarnates? What is the "soul"? Do we have the same personality from life to life? Other questions that have surely arisen in the course of your research also demand an answer. This final chapter may help you to bring all of your research experiences into focus.

At the outset, you should understand that there is a secret teaching that is to be found in the hidden traditions of the genuine sages of humanity from time immemorial. These include, but are not limited to, the Ger-Maa of Ancient Egypt, the Prophets of Biblical Israel, the Christian and Pagan Gnostics, the Hindu and Buddhist philosophic yogis, the Taoists of China and the Sufis of Islam.

These *Reincarnation Cards* are intended not only to help you to recall details of so-called incarnations, but also to awaken your intuition to the full, leading to a direct insight into what is ultimately *real*, behind all such phenomena. You will then *know* that, as consciousness itself, you are *essentially* identical to the Logos or Brahman, the One Cosmic Mind. All "births," "deaths," "personalities" and "incarnations," although endlessly fascinating to study, are ephemeral phenomena of no *ultimate* significance other than to guide you to *discover for yourself* this final, complete understanding.

This book repeatedly refers to incarnations that you "appear" to experience "vicariously" through the agency of quite different and distinct, "projected," "emanated," or "temporary" personalities. You may now appreciate that the same is true of your current apparent incarnation: that indeed it *is* only *apparent*.

One purpose of these terms was to help you to shed the common belief, normally held with hypnotic force, that you are an unchanging individual soul-personality wandering through the incarnations in search of "enlightenment." For so long as you believe yourself to be "a seeker on the Path," you are condemned to stay there, going round in circles, until you realize who you really are and have always been. You will then *know* that there is no "Path" and there is no "Goal"; there is no "progress" and there is no "spiritual evolution" to a finer and loftier state of being, other than in seeming. These are all an illusion.

The final truth is that there is, and can be, only the One Mind, the ultimate Self of All, in an Eternal Now, and you are *That*. You are not an insignificant mortal "creature" in a vast, external universe. On the contrary, the universe and all of "creation" are in you. The question is, How did this misunderstanding come to be? By creating "time" and by focusing attention increasingly on an infinitesimally tiny part of your

Infinite Being, in the course of transition to the vastly-shrunken "individual" level, you have progressively forgotten who you really are.

The virtually infinite number of tiny, egoic minds that you mentally create within yourself are a means by which you, the Cosmic Self, experience limited existences like those of a flower, a whale, a god, or a star. But each of these minuscule, egoic minds, owing to the intuited sense of unlimited freedom and selfhood that it derives from its Source, mistakenly believes itself to be entirely independent. In the human, it erects a psychological barrier round itself that unimaginably reduces its super-conscious awareness of its true identity as Cosmic Mind. It thereby limits itself to a vastly diminished perception of an apparent existence in a single "projected personality." That personality, your everyday self, appears to be immured in a particular time-and-space projected mental framework. This constitutes a so-called "incarnation."

By creatively walling itself off from what it believes to be "others," the tiny, self-isolated egoic mind has condemned itself to suffer from a basic fault in its perception, a form of spiritual or psychic blindness. Such a fundamental failure of the reasoning process is, literally, insanity. This false, dualist-materialist belief in a totally independent individual self and in the centrality and preeminence of the ego, gives rise to fear of imagined "others," to an urge to accumulate at their expense and to assert power over them, who are misperceived as totally different from oneself. This simple misperception has the most unfortunate and far-reaching consequences.

Owing to the mental block or fence erected round itself by the egoic mind, the imprisoned, now insane, person believes in the separate reality of an illusory something apparently outside, called "matter." This "matter" is *supposed* to exist entirely independent of the observer. It is thought to be capable of being examined at arm's length and studied with a completely impersonal "objectivity." Believing that "things" are totally separate from and independent of each other and from him or her, the insane person is always puzzled by the simultaneity of events and the ubiquitousness of Mind revealed by the great pioneers of quantum physics, as recorded in Chapter Two, *The Evidence*.

Unable otherwise to account for consciousness, the insane materialist simply *assumes* that it *must be* a chemical secretion of, and therefore limited to, the individual human brain. This leads him or her to conceive of "things" as "outside," suspended in "space" that appear to be stable but that somehow manage mysteriously to "change" through "time" (see "The Illusion of Change" in Chapter Two). This dualist-materialist misinterpretation of reality reinforces a strongly held, but false belief in the actuality of the egoic mind, or personality, as apparently confined within a human body.

You are not the body nor do you *have* a body. You are not *a* soul, separate and apart from anything or anyone else. You are pure Consciousness Itself. Nothing is known, or can be known, other than in and as consciousness. *All* that you perceive is perceived *within* you and is your very Self.

As the Cosmic Self, or Atman, you look upon each incarnate emanation not only impersonally, but also *both* sequentially *and* simultaneously. You grasp the entire universe and everything in it, past, present and future, through and through, within the Self, in one vast vision, one all-timed fixity. That all-embracing insight is the total manifestation of your true nature. For an "individual" fully to understand this, and personally to realize it, is enlightenment.

The enlightened person clearly perceives pure consciousness as the ultimate, timeless Reality that underlies and animates all transient appearances. He or she clearly discriminates between the temporarily existent and the permanently Real, and sees that although the constantly changing world is clearly *outside the body*, it is just as obviously, including the transitory body itself, *inside the mind*. The common failure of people to make this simple distinction is due to confusing the mind with the brain and, above all, to the existence of what has been aptly called the "skin-encapsulated ego," which acts as an opaque barrier to transcendental perception. The result is their sheer *inability* to see that All is One, and that nothing is truly *real* other than the Self.

Having overcome the ego-block that formerly shut him or her off from the "rest of the world," the now-sane person directly perceives that this Cosmic Consciousness is a universal field in which all "creatures" and "things," including him- or herself as "individuals," arise in consciousness, exist in consciousness, and dissolve in consciousness — while forever remaining, in essence, that pure, timeless Consciousness-in-Itself. Birthless and death-less, they now *know* that they are not transitory, limited individuals forever separate and apart from each other, as they formerly believed themselves to be. Their ultimate, immortal Being *is* the Atman, the Cosmic Self.

With the dawning of this knowledge, there comes a radically profound, revelatory shift in the center of consciousness, from the personal to the universal. They now regard all of "creation" as sacred and all "creatures," human and non-human, animate and inanimate, terrestrial or "alien," as their very Self. Hence they are totally incapable of wilfully inflicting harm on "others." *There is no "other"* in this or any world or universe. This supreme Self-awareness is Love. This, at long last, is sanity.

When the wall that the egoic mind has erected between itself and "others" falls away, it will finally know what Jesus meant when he said "I and my Father are One." (John 10:30) and "The Kingdom of God is within you." (Luke 17:21) In the Old Testament, the psalmist sang, "Be still and know that I am God." (Psalm 46:10) In the Vedanta, Atman (Cosmic Self) and Brahman (the Absolute; Cosmic Mind) are One.

From this lofty standpoint, there is no "sin" and there is no "punishment," divine or otherwise. The *only* sin, the Original Sin, is that you have forgotten who you are. This forgetfulness of your transcendental Being is the only Fall from Grace; there is no other.

It will now be clear why these "ear-whispered teachings" were withheld for so long and were revealed to only the most tried and tested disciples, who were always sworn to secrecy and who, in some cultures, might even be put to death for breaking their solemn oath. This liberating doctrine would inevitably be misunderstood and twisted to justify the worst acts of the insane, demoniacal humans who appear in every age and in every society. It would be eagerly seized upon by unenlightened egoic minds who, considering themselves to be free of ultimate responsibility for their actions, would perceive it as a licence to do anything they might wish to do without fear of Karmic retribution.

Such as they fail to realize that, from the point of view of the "incarnate individual" who is self-locked into the insane, egoistic belief system, there *are* sinful acts and those acts *do* reap Karmic consequences. Purgatories and Hells, albeit *ultimately* unreal, *do* exist for those who believe that, as individuals, they can do as they please to others without incurring a personally painful, but always just, requital that is appropriate to their level of understanding.

"A little knowledge is a dangerous thing." The wisdom of this saying is constantly being demonstrated by the time-bound and space-fettered insane, who may have had a glimpse of their divine origin in the One Cosmic Self, but who have not personally realized this metaphysics and thereby recovered their original sanity. Impelled by fear, lust and greed, and believing themselves to be divine or divinely inspired, they are capable of inflicting the most appalling atrocities on those whom they still mistakenly perceive to be "others." Confident in their misconceived "messianic immunity," they stop at nothing to achieve their grossly selfish, material goals and can put thousands of the innocent to death without a qualm.

Alexander the Great believed himself to be a god, born of a god, and had himself proclaimed a god. The murderous conqueror Attila the Hun was followed by Genghis Khan and Tamerlane, the self-styled "Man of Destiny" Napoleon and, in the twentieth century, by Hitler, Stalin and Mao, each of whom slaughtered millions. Such sick, swollen egos, believing themselves, as individuals, to have been divinely chosen or ordained, are to be seen strutting on the world stage today. Humankind have learned little over the millennia.

Despite these continuing dangers, the time has passed when there was anything to be gained by secrecy. On the contrary, from the purely human point of view, it is increasingly urgent for as many as possible, as soon as possible, to become aware of Who they really are, and to be alert to the activities of the insane majority. You may be few in number, but at this moment in history your leavening influence on the mass of humanity may be the only hope for the survival of humankind on this planet.

This notwithstanding, in the final analysis it is in the very nature of this "God"-dreamed universe to BE what It IS. All ideas of evolution are time-constrained, hence an illusion. Those who believe that the world is progressively evolving, growing toward some distant, sublime goal, have still not entirely shed their materialistic outlook. The Real world is not one thing and themselves another. They are *One*, forever *here* and *now*. All so-called events, like waves splashing and playing together on the surface of the sea are, in and of themselves, of no significance. Such forms simply appear only instantly to disappear. All apparent changes take place at only the most superficial level. "But if only they knew, they are already in Nirvana, for in Noble Wisdom, all things are in Nirvana from the beginning." (Lankavatara Sutra) Beneath the restless waves the vast and silent Ocean of Being remains what It IS and has always been. Hence whatever apparently happens to the world or to humankind ultimately is unimportant. To outward seeming, this imagined world and all its "time"- and "space"-bound "creatures" will inevitably dissolve and disappear.

Thus shall you think of all this fleeting world,
A star at dawn, a bubble in a stream,
A flash of lightning in a summer cloud,
A flickering lamp, a phantom,
And a dream . . . (Diamond Sutra)

But You, Cosmic Mind, are forever.

Afterword

The authors designed and wrote *Reincarnation Cards — Awakening Far Memory* out of a sincere desire to enable people to find themselves and thereby to fulfill the purpose for which they chose to be here. Given the nature of this project, you are very likely to have evoked any number of far memories of apparent incarnations. Other experiences of a psychic nature also may have been generated by your research activities.

The authors would be most interested to receive your accounts of any such elicited material as well as any suggestions you may have that might lead to improvement in future editions of this work.

Please feel free to communicate with the authors through:

Ger Maa Publishers
P. O. Box 62064
8060 Paphos, Cyprus (CY)
Website: www.reincarnationcards.com
Email: info@reincarnationcards.com

The confidentiality of all such communications will be respected and messages will be relayed to the authors.

"There is no death of anyone, but only an appearance, even as there is no birth of any, save only in seeming. The change from being to becoming seems to be birth, and the change from becoming to being seems to be death, but in reality no one is ever born, nor does one ever die ... Being is ever the same, its only change being motion and rest ... the whole becomes parts and parts become whole in the oneness of the all."

Apollonius of Tyana (1st century CE)

❋ ❋ ❋

"No individual entity is ever born. There does not exist any cause which can produce it. The supreme truth is that nothing is ever born."

Gaudapada, 8th century CE (Karika, III-48)

❋ ❋ ❋

"There is no dissolution, no birth, none in bondage, none aspiring for wisdom, no seeker of liberation, and none liberated. This is the absolute truth."

Gaudapada, 8th century CE (Karika, II—32)

Glossary

From time immemorial, philosophers have enjoined on us the need to define our terms. Accordingly, this section defines a number of terms *as used in this book*. The usages herein may not conform to dictionary definitions. Words in italics in any definition are an indication that they are defined separately and listed in alphabetical order elsewhere in the Glossary.

Absolute – Ultimate *Reality*. See *Brahman*.

Antedate – Precede in time.

Assumption – That which is taken for granted, without proof or logical reason. See *Fallacy, Matter*.

"Atlantis" – A legendary island in the Atlantic Ocean described by Plato in the *Timaeus* and the *Critias*, reportedly overwhelmed by the sea in approximately 9600 BCE. "Atlantis" is a symbol that stands for an earlier worldwide civilization destroyed by a *cataclysmic* event. See *Deluge, NEO*.

Atman – The Higher *Self* or *Overself;* also pure *awareness, consciousness* without an object. The "Self" aspect of *Brahman*, or Ultimate *Reality* with which Atman is identical. See *Identity*.

Awareness – *Reality, Consciousness, Atman, Brahman, Essence*. The ultimate *Being* or be-ness.

Being – See *Essence, Awareness.*

BCE – Before the Common Era (previously BC).

BP – Before the Present.

Brahman – *Logos, Absolute.* Pure *Consciousness, Universal* or *Cosmic Mind*-in-Itself; the impersonal aspect of *Reality* as it is in Itself that may be experienced as a *Self* through *Atman.*

CE – Of the Common Era (previously AD).

Cataclysm (Greek, Kataklysmós, "Deluge") – An overwhelming flood.

Consciousness – *Awareness*; the pure *essence* of *being,* beyond time, space and both external and internal *phenomenal* experience. See *Logos, Brahman, Atman, Cosmic Mind,* "*God.*"

Cosmic Mind – *Universal Mind*; the mental continuum, itself not directly perceptible, that underlies all appearances and may therefore be said to be indirectly perceptible in all things as their *substantial essence.* See also *Logos, Brahman, Atman, Being, Reality,* "*God.*"

Creationism – The belief that a separate, individual creator *God* made all things (creatures) out of nothing at a specific time in the past. See "*God,*" *God.*

Credentialism – The doctrine and practice that a person with formal *credentials,* especially one who has been admitted into the *Establishment,* is the only person who has a valid opinion and is inherently more worthy to be heard from than someone who lacks them.

Credentials – Formal testimonials indicating that a person is entitled to belief or credit; required for admission to the *Scientistic Establishment* (usually a doctorate).

Culture – Body of customs and civilization of a particular time or people.

Deluge – A flood, e.g., the "Great Flood of All," caused by either an impact on the ocean or the near passage of a *Near Earth Object (NEO)*, as a consequence of which "the springs of the great deep burst forth and the floodgates of the heavens were opened" (Genesis 7:11). Such an event totally destroyed an advanced, worldwide, maritime civilization and all but exterminated the human species in one indescribably terrible *cataclysm* in about 9600 BCE.

Deluge, Ogygian – Said to have preceded the legendary Greek flood of Deucalion by hundreds of years. "The planet Venus underwent great changes in its diameter, its color, its shape and its course" (Varro). Implies the near approach or impact of an *NEO*. Possibly the "Great Flood of All" of Plato.

Dogma – A teaching, usually with the connotation of narrow, opinionated, unyielding rigidity and conservatism.

Dowsing – A method of gaining access to the unconscious mind to obtain help in locating objects, so-called "substances" such as minerals or water, or forgotten memories, using such instruments as divining rods or *pendulums*. May include "map"-dowsing with a pendulum.

Dualism – The belief that *things exist* as *matter* totally separate and apart from each other, with no underlying mental connection or continuum; the "finger philosophy" that deems what can be felt with the fingers as a suitable criterion for ultimate *reality*. On the so-called individual level, it considers people to exist totally independently of each other and of an external world, with no underlying unity in *consciousness*. See *Non-locality, Quantum Physics, Insanity, Monism.*

Egoic Mind – The *persona*; the temporary personality or apparent individuality that is projected or emanated by the *Higher Self* into what is *vicariously* experienced as an *incarnation* at a particular period and place. See *Reincarnation, Soul.*

Ephemeral – Short lived, transitory, lasting for only a short period of time.

Essence – Pure *Being; Consciousness; Awareness. That which IS* at the core of all *existence.* The ultimate *substance* of the obviously existent but actually unreal physical universe.

Establishment – Social group exercising authority or influence and characteristically resisting change, e.g., the *Scientistic Establishment.*

Establishment, Scientistic – The hierarchy of *materialist, reductionist* scientists who have created an orthodox *dogma* of received scientific doctrine to which all scientists must adhere or be expelled from the scientistic "priesthood" as *heretics.*

Eternal Now – The ultimate state of timeless, spaceless *Being* in which every event is perceived to be happening at once. An ancient *insight* supported, *inter alia,* by both the *Vedanta* and *quantum physics.* See also *Logos, Non-locality, Superluminal, Brahman, "God."*

Existence – Comprises changeable, perceptible *phenomena* that are themselves unreal, but that are manifested and animated by the underlying *Reality* which is Itself not otherwise directly perceptible by the senses.

Fallacy – Mistaken belief, faulty reasoning, misleading argument; sophistry; forcible argument that is really illogical; a delusion. See *Assumption, Matter.*

Far Memory – Recall to one's present-day individual egoic conscious awareness of apparent events and life experiences stored in the *Atman,* the *Overself,* or Higher, *Cosmic Self,* that are not readily attributable to one's current life experience and that may fairly be presumed to be valid recollections of episodes *vicariously* experienced through other emanated or *projected personalities* in other so-called *incarnations.*

Ger Maa (Classical Egyptian) – The Silent One of Truth, i.e., the *sage.* Combination of two hieroglyphs, Ger (silence or silent one) and Maa (Truth). See *True Philosopher.*

Gestalt Switch – Also known as a paradigm shift. The sudden transition in understanding from one *paradigm* or belief system to another, whereby the same universe is perceived but in a new and quite different way; e.g., a change from a *dualist, materialist* view of a world external to one's body and *egoic mind* to one that is *monist* and *mentalist*, where it is recognized that Mind is everywhere and that the reverse is actually true — the body and the universe are in the Mind.

Gnosis (Greek, "knowledge") – Ultimate knowledge of *That which Is* by direct *insight*. See *Vedanta, Sage, "God," Brahman, Logos.*

"God" – *Brahman, Absolute Being* and the *Reality* that underlies and animates all phenomenal appearances. Also the *Logos, Cosmic or Universal Mind*, within which all *things* and events appear to arise, to be sustained for a time, and to dissolve. Timeless and impersonal in Itself, as the very *essence* of Selfhood, It is *Atman*. It is also pure *consciousness* or *awareness* of all events in all times and places within Itself, both sequentially and simultaneously. Infinitely both immanent and transcendent, "God" *is* the universe. See *Eternal Now.*

God – A supposed superhuman entity, a "creator" who is believed to have made the universe and all *things*. To be worshipped as the sole possessor of ultimate, divine power. See *Creationism.*

Heretic (Greek, Hairésis "opinion") – A freethinker; a person who chooses to form his or her own independent opinions rather than passively to accept *Establishment dogma.*

Identity – Absolute sameness; oneness; *Atman*; "Know Thyself and Thou Wilt Know the Universe and the Gods" (Temple of Apollo at Delphi); "I am That I Am." (Exodus 3:13) "You are not the body. You are Consciousness itself, the eternal Witness, and free." (Astavakra Samhita XV–4); "It is through your ignorance alone that the universe exists. In reality, you are One. There is no individual self or Supreme Self other than you." (Astavakra Samhita XV–16) See *Self, Brahman, Logos, Essence, Being, Reality, Overself, "God," Awareness, Atman, Consciousness.*

Incarnation – See *Reincarnation.*

Insanity – Disordered reason; may include clinically certifiable psychoses; the normal condition of *dualist, materialist* humankind, characterized by belief in the separate and independent existence of a world external to the body, composed of an *assumed* something called *matter;* and by the belief that "you" and "I" are separate individuals who must forever compete against each other for food, shelter, mates and status. This leads to fear and a felt need to control or to dominate assumed "others" by physical force; the perennial source of such characteristically human behavior as aggressive wars, theft, pillage, rape and murder.

Insight – Direct perception with understanding; a "seeing through" outer appearances. See *Sage.*

Intelligent Design – As the universe is alive, conscious and mental, all *things* are intimately interwoven, both individually and collectively, in an infinite complexity, the whole united in a vast cosmic harmony. Universal *consciousness* implies universal intelligence, hence the concept of intelligent design. Not to be confused with *creationism,* a common misunderstanding that is promoted by both *scientistic* and creationist *materialists.*

Inter alia (Latin) – Among other things.

Intuition – Immediate apprehension of a truth by direct *insight,* without reasoning.

Logos (Greek, "word") – The One *Cosmic Mind* or *Reality* in which all *things* and events exist as ideas but are themselves non-material and unreal. See *Brahman, Essence, "God."*

Materialism – A *dogmatic* belief based on the *assumption* that a hypothetical something called *matter* is *real;* involves a rejection of all spiritual values and a refusal to recognize the underlying unity of all *things* (the universe) in *consciousness.* See *Insanity.*

Matter – A term invented to account for the apparently separate *existence* of an *assumed* external world as if it were forever separate and apart from the observer. The greatest of all *fallacies.* Assumes that only physically detectible *things* are *real.* See *Quantum Physics.*

Mentalism – Declares that the universe is alive, conscious and mental; that *Mind,* not *matter,* is all that is; that all *things* are wholly and entirely mental things, ideas in *Cosmic Mind.* It teaches that all that one knows, or can ever know, is known only in and as consciousness, the ultimate *reality. Matter* may be said to exist as *things,* but it and they are ultimately unreal. See *True Philosopher, Sage.*

Metaphysics – The branch of philosophy that deals with first principles, including such concepts as *being, existence, reality, substance, consciousness, identity,* space, time, etc. See *Sage.*

Mind – See *Cosmic Mind, Atman, Logos, Brahman, "God," Identity.*

Monism – The basic principle that all existence (i.e., the universe) is, by definition, One; may be conceived as either "material" or "mental." See *Mentalism.*

Monism, Mental – The understanding that there is only the one *Reality, Cosmic Mind* or *Brahman,* That which always IS, and that all things and experiences perceived within It are wholly and entirely mental. They may be said to exist physically but, of themselves, they are unreal except in their timeless, immortal *essence.* See *Mentalism, Matter, Existence, Identity.*

"Mu" – An extensive, legendary land area in the Pacific Ocean that may equate to Sundaland, much of which was overwhelmed by the sea perhaps at approximately the same time as was *"Atlantis,"* but possibly much earlier in a *deluge* called the Flood of Manu.

Mystical – Refers to inner, psychic experience; not to be confused with "mysterious." At its best, a *transcendental* experience of unity with *Atman/Brahman/Logos* through meditation, contemplation, or continuously pursued *insightful* understanding of *reality* that underlies daily conscious experience; in theological terms, involving union with "*God.*" See *Sage.*

NB (Latin, "Nota Bene") – Note well.

NEO – Near Earth Object, such as a large comet or asteroid the impact or close passage of which has on numerous occasions brought a geological era or epoch to a catastrophic end.

Non-locality – The principle, as revealed by research into *quantum physics*, that everything in the universe is subliminally connected in a continuum with everything else; that an action that affects one part of the universe affects all in a non-local way, instantaneously (i.e., in *Absolute Mind* or "*God,*" everything in the universe and all events are actually happening at once). They normally appear to us as positioned in space and in a time sequence only because of our own physical four-dimensional, perceptual limitations. See *Eternal Now.*

OOPARTS – Out-of-place artifacts, e.g., a fabricated gold chain found embedded in a lump of coal dating from the Carboniferous Period of the Palaeozoic Era, 286 to 360 million years BP — one of countless examples (see Cremo & Thompson, Corliss et al.).

Overself – See *Atman, Identity.*

Paradigm (Greek, parádeigma, "example") – A model; a complete belief system. Can be modified by a *Gestalt Switch*.

Paranormal – That field of study that lies outside the range of normal scientific investigation, beyond what should occur if only the known laws of cause and effect are operating.

Past-life regression – Induction, often by means of hypnosis, by a psychiatrist, clinical psychologist or past-life therapist, of apparent reincarnational *far memories*.

Pendulum – Body suspended from a fixed point so as to swing freely. May be used as a divining rod for *dowsing* purposes.

Persona (Latin, "mask" used by the player of a role) – The personality created by the *Self* and emanated or projected into apparent *incarnation*. See *Projected Personality, Egoic Mind, Soul*.

Phenomenon (a) – That which is perceived or observed; the changeable *existent* as opposed to the changeless *real*.

Philosophy – Love, study and pursuit of wisdom, especially that which deals with ultimate *reality*. See *Academic Philosopher, True Philosopher, Sage*.

Philosopher, Academic – A claimed philosopher who, often with the best of intentions, has failed to overcome egoic tendencies and remains trapped in a *dualist materialism*. Consequently believes that everything is "relative" and that *absolute* truth or *reality* is unknowable. As a *credentialed* member of the *Establishment*, puts him- or herself forward as a "professional philosopher."

Philosopher, True – A lover of wisdom who is devoted to the search for fundamental truth. Not to be confused with the *Academic Philosopher* of the *Establishment*. See *Sage*.

Projected Personality – *Egoic mind* projected or emanated by the *Higher Self* into incarnation, where it temporarily assumes individual characteristics unique to that lifetime's experience. Also the *Soul, Persona*.

Protohistory – The unofficial history of the human species as largely derived from evidence found by many serious, non-*establishment* anthropological researchers (see Brophy, Hancock, West, Schoch, et al.), from innumerable legendary accounts, and from one's own *far memory*, whether spontaneous or induced.

Quantum Physics – Body of research by the most advanced physical scientists into the true nature of so-called *matter* at the deepest (quantum) level that has revealed, *inter alia*, that "there is no matter as such!" (Max Planck); that all is Mind (Sir James Jeans, Sir Arthur Eddington, Erwin Schrödinger); that "before and after" time is only an illusion (Albert Einstein, Louis de Broglie); that all *things* are interconnected and that instantaneous communication takes place *superluminally* between particles separated by the entire universe, i.e., everything is happening at once (John Bell). "In a word, quantum physics declares that All is One in the undivided totality of the universe itself." (David Bohm) See Chapter Two "The Evidence."

Real – Actual; changeless and forever true. See *Being, Consciousness, Reality.*

Reality – That which always IS, changeless *Being* that underlies ever-changing *phenomenal* appearances. The actual *substance* of the universe as opposed to an *assumed matter.* See *Essence, Brahman, Logos, "God," Identity.*

Reductionism – The tendency to diminish; to reduce any concept to make it comply with the *assumption* that all *things* are composed of something called *matter* by eliminating all non-material aspects or qualities from consideration.

Reincarnation – The emanation or projection of a temporary personality, *persona* or *egoic mind,* into a *vicariously* experienced apparent world.

Resonance – An *intuition,* a sense of a trace memory of another *incarnation;* a feeling of attunement with a psychic impression.

Sage – A person of profound wisdom, a *true philosopher* who has personally realized his or her *metaphysics.* A "seer of the *essence*" who has gained the supreme *insight* into *Reality* and experienced the oceanic *consciousness.* See *Atman, Brahman, Logos, Essence, Identity.*

Scientism – The *materialist, reductionist dogma* that the only acceptable evidence is that which neatly fits into the framework of science that has been recognized and accepted by the Scientific (*Scientistic*) *Establishment*. All new evidence must pass through a scientistic, pseudo-scientific screen to be considered as valid.

Scientists, non-quantum – Scientists of an older school who have not advanced beyond a basic belief in the actuality of so-called *matter* as laid down by Descartes and Newton in the seventeenth century CE and their followers.

Self, Higher – See *Atman, Identity.*

Soul – The so-called spiritual or immaterial part; a supposed separate and independent entity believed to have been created in time, that is assumed to be immortal — a belief that derives from an intuitive realization of one's true *identity* with the immortal *Self, Overself,* or *Atman,* that Itself is One with the All, *Cosmic Mind,* or "*God.*" See *Egoic Mind, Persona.*

Synchronicity – Meaningful coincidence — a notable concurrence of events without apparent causal connection that nevertheless appears to be meaningful to the experiencer. To the materialist all coincidences are purely accidental relationships. To the mentalist, there is no such thing as a purely accidental relationship; all things and events are subliminally interconnected. As one's *insight* grows, more and more synchronicities are seen to occur.

Substance – That which lies under appearances. True substance is not *matter,* as defined in the dictionaries, but the underlying *reality, consciousness* or *Mind*, beyond and behind the appearances that are presented to the senses. See *Essence*.

Superluminal – Beyond the speed of light. Implies universal simultaneity. See *Quantum Physics, Non-locality, Eternal Now.*

That which IS – See *Absolute, Essence, Eternal Now, "God," Identity, Logos.*

Thing – That which appears, that exists, but is found by analysis to be ultimately unreal although *substantially real* in *essence*. See *Substance, Matter, Existence.*

Transcendental – Describes that which goes beyond, that rises above all *assumed* human limitations.

Universal Mind – See *Cosmic Mind, Brahman, Logos, "God."*

Vedanta – System of *monistic philosophy* based on the Upanishads. See *Gnosis.*

Vicarious – Deputed, delegated, acting: the means whereby one experiences incarnation as an emanated or projected personality.

"In you, who are the infinite ocean, let the waves of the universe rise and fall according to their own nature. That means no gain or loss to you."

Astavakra Samhita XV–11

"Jesus said, 'What you look forward to has already come, but you do not recognize it.' . . . 'The Kingdom of the Father is spread out upon the earth and people do not see it.'"

Gospel of Thomas

✾ ✾ ✾

"Although the Logos is forever, people ever fail to understand, both before and after hearing it."

Herákleitos, 6th century BCE

✾ ✾ ✾

"People are deceived by failing to recognize what is obvious."

Herákleitos, 6th century BCE

Selected Bibliography

A. REINCARNATION

1. Andrews, Ted, *How to Uncover Your Past Lives*. St. Paul MN: Llewellyn, 1992.

2. Bernstein, Morey, *The Search for Bridey Murphy*. NY: Doubleday, 1950. Efforts to "debunk" this case have been refuted by Dr. C.J. Ducasse, writing in item (10) below.

3. Cerminara, Dr. Gina, *Many Mansions*. NY: William Sloane Assoc., 1950. A psychologist examines the philosophy underlying past life research, karma and health.

4. Cerminara, Dr. Gina, *The World Within*. NY: William Sloane Assoc., 1957. A psychologist studies the implications of reincarnation. How does it change one's attitude to life? The body? Sex? Race? Religion?

5. Cerminara, Dr. Gina, *Many Lives, Many Loves*. NY: William Sloane Assoc., 1963. An eloquent and inspiring treatment of love from the reincarnation perspective.

6. Cockell, Jenny, *Across Time and Death: A Mother's Search for her Past-Life Children*. NY: Fireside Books, 1994. The true verified story of how Jenny Cockell actually found the still-living children that she had left behind in Ireland in a previous incarnation.

7. Cockell, Jenny, *Past Lives, Future Lives*. NY: Fireside Books, 1996. Records her "memories" of both past and future incarnations.

8. Cranston, Sylvia & Carey Williams, *Reincarnation: A New Horizon in Science, Religion and Society*. NY: Julian Press (Crown Pubs), 1984. A wide-ranging survey, bringing together the work of scientists, theologians, social historians, psychologists. A most comprehensive and practical book.

9. Danelek, J. Allan, *Mystery of Reincarnation; The Evidence and Analysis of Rebirth*. St. Paul, MN: Llewellyn, 2005.

10. Ebon, Martin (Ed), *Reincarnation in the Twentieth Century*. NY: New American Library, 1970. Records a number of documented case histories of reincarnation.

11. Finkelstein, Dr. Adrian, *Your Past Lives and the Healing Process*. Farmingdale NY: Coleman Publishing, 1985. A psychiatrist looks at reincarnation and spiritual healing.

12. Fiore, Dr. Edith, *You Have Been Here Before*. NY: Coward, McCann & Geoghegan, 1978. A clinical psychologist presents case histories of reincarnation from her practice, with much about curing phobias and physical disabilities carried over from previous incarnations.

13. Hall, Manly P., *Reincarnation: The Cycle of Necessity*. Los Angeles, CA: Philosophical Research Society, 1971.

14. Holzer, Hans, *Born Again: The Truth About Reincarnation*. Garden City, NY: Doubleday, 1970.

15. McClain, Florence W., *A Practical Guide to Past Life Regression.* St. Paul MN: Llewellyn, 1985. A useful practical manual for the aspiring reincarnation researcher.

16. Snow, Dr. Chet B., *Mass Dreams of the Future.* Crest Park CA: Deep Forest Press, 1989. A startling examination of future incarnations. A superb merging of age-old traditions with the meticulous research of the late Dr. Helen Wambach (see item 23 below) on future events.

17. Stevenson, Dr. Ian, *Twenty Cases Suggestive of Reincarnation.* Charlottesville: U. of Virginia Press, 1966. Dr. Stevenson is former Carlson Professor of Psychiatry at the University of Virginia Medical School and former chairman of the Department. He has over four thousand carefully investigated cases of reincarnation in his files. His book *Where Reincarnation and Biology Intersect* (see item 19 below) has put the final nail in the coffin of the skeptics, deniers and doubters of the reality of the reincarnation phenomenon.

18. Stevenson, Dr. Ian, *Children Who Remember Past Lives.* Charlottesville: U. of Virginia Press, 1987/1992. Dr. Stevenson provides case studies of children's reincarnational memories.

19. Stevenson, Dr. Ian, *Where Reincarnation and Biology Intersect.* Westport CT: Praeger, 1997. This most important work is a condensation of a much longer one titled *Reincarnation and Biology: A Contribution to the Etiology*

of Birthmarks and Birth Defects, a medical monograph with extensive documentation, references, tables, footnotes and photographic evidence (as also in the condensed version). Individual chapters in this abbreviated, scholarly work cover such topics as "Birthmarks Corresponding to Wounds Verified by Informants' Memories" (Ch. 5); "Birthmarks Corresponding to Wounds Verified by Medical Records" (Ch. 6); "Birthmarks Corresponding to Surgical Wounds and Other Skin Lesions on Deceased Persons" (Ch. 7); "Birthmarks Corresponding to other Types of Wounds or Marks on Deceased Persons" (Ch. 8); "Nevi (moles) Corresponding to Wounds or Other Marks on Deceased Persons" (Ch. 9); "Some Correlates of Birthmarks Attributed to Previous Lives" (Ch. 14); "The Interpretations of Birthmarks Related to Previous Lives" (Ch. 15); "Internal Diseases Related to Previous Lives" (Ch. 21); "Abnormalities of Pigmentation that May Derive from Previous Lives" (Ch. 22); "Physiques, Postures, Gestures and Other Involuntary Movements Related to Previous Lives" (Ch. 23); etc. This is the ideal book for anyone who still doubts the truth of the reincarnation phenomenon.

20. Sutphen, Dick, *You Were Born to be Together.* NY: Pocket Books, 1976. Prominent psychic and past-life researcher examines how love and karma reunite the same couples life after life. Case histories.

21. Sutphen, Dick, *Past Lives, Future Loves.* NY: Pocket Books, 1978.

22. Talbot, Michael, *Your Past Lives: A Reincarnation Handbook.* NY: Ballantine, 1987. An explicit, step-by-step guide for remembering and exploring past lives. Also recounts his own spontaneous memories of previous incarnations.

23. Wambach, Dr. Helen, *Reliving Past Lives.* NY: Harper & Row (Barnes & Noble), 1984. Clinical psychologist presents the evidence of over one thousand hypnosis-induced past life recalls.

24. Weiss, Dr. Brian L., *Same Soul, Many Bodies.* London: Piatkus, 2004. Psychiatrist explores future as well as past-life experiences of his patients.

25. Weiss, Dr. Brian L., *Many Lives, Many Masters.* NY: Fireside, 1988. Psychiatrist recounts the case history of a patient who recalled past-life traumas that seemed to hold the key to her recurring nightmares and anxiety attacks. Using past-life therapy, Dr. Weiss was able to cure his patient. Dr. Weiss has written several other books on the subject of his experiences with patients involving the cure of past-life-generated phobias.

26. Williston, Dr. Glenn and Judith Johnstone, *Discovering Your Past Lives,* London: Harper Collins, 1998. Dr. Williston is a clinical psychologist who has successfully

developed the protocol for regression therapy. This book contains many insights into the greater self and its incarnate manifestations; a treatise on spiritual growth through a knowledge of past lifetimes.

B. GENERAL

1. Allan, D.S. & J.B. Delair, *Cataclysm! Compelling Evidence of a Cosmic Cataclysm in 9500 B.C.* Rochester, VT: Bear & Co., 1997.

2. Atlantis Rising (Eds.), *The Search for Lost Origins.* Livingston, MT: Atlantis Rising Books, 1996.

3. Baigent, Michael, *Ancient Traces: Mysteries in Ancient and Early History.* London & New York: Viking (Penguin Books), 1998.

4. Bauval, Robert & Adrian Gilbert, *The Orion Mystery.* London: Heinemann, 1994.

5. Bauval, Robert, & Graham Hancock, *Keeper of Genesis: A Quest for the Hidden Legacy of Mankind.* London: Heinemann, 1996.

6. Black, Jeremy & Anthony Green, *Gods, Demons and Symbols of Ancient Mesopotamia.* London: British Museum, 1992.

7. Bohm, David, *Causality and Chance in Modern Physics.* London: Routledge & Kegan Paul, 1957/1984.

8. Bohm, David, *Wholeness and the Implicate Order.*

London: Routledge & Kegan Paul, 1980/1983.

9. Brophy, Thomas G., *The Origin Map: Discovery of a Prehistoric, Megalithic, Astrophysical Map and Sculpture of the Universe.* Lincoln, NE: iUniverse/Writers Club, 2002.

10. Brunton, Paul, *The Hidden Teaching Beyond Yoga.* London: Rider & Company, 1941.

11. Brunton, Paul, *The Wisdom of the Overself.* NY: E.P. Dutton & Co., 1943.

12. Budge, E.A. Wallis, *The Teaching of Amen-Em-Apt, Son of Kanekht.* London: Martin Hopkinson & Co., Covent Garden, 1924.

13. Bucke, Richard M., *Cosmic Consciousness.* NY: EP Dutton, 1969.

14. Burgos Stone, Hector, *Amáraka, Mundo Sin Tiempo.* Guayaquil, Ecuador: Editorial del Pacifico, undated.

15. Cabrera Darquea, Javier, *El Mensaje de las Piedras Grabadas de ICA* (The Message of the Engraved Stones of ICA). Peru: Intisol, 1976.

16. Childress, David Hatcher, *Technology of the Gods: The Incredible Sciences of the Ancients.* Kempton, Illinois: Adventures Unlimited, 2000.

17. Childress, David Hatcher, *Vimana Aircraft of Ancient India and Atlantis.* Stelle, Illinois: Adventures Unlimited Press, 1991.

18. Corliss, William R., *Ancient Infrastructure — Remarkable Roads, Mines, Walls, Mounds, Stone Circles.* Glen Arm, Maryland: The Sourcebook Project, 1999.

19. Corliss, William R., *Ancient Man: A Handbook of Puzzling Artifacts.* Glen Arm, Maryland: The Sourcebook Project, 1978.

20. Corliss, William R., *Archaeological Anomalies: Small Artifacts; Bone, Stone, Metal Artifacts, Footprints, High Technology.* Glen Arm, Maryland: The Sourcebook Project, 2003.

21. Corliss, William R., *Science Frontiers: Some Anomalies and Curiosities of Nature.* Glen Arm, Maryland: The Sourcebook Project, 1994.

22. Corliss, William R., *Science Frontiers II: More Anomalies and Curiosities of Nature.* Glen Arm, Maryland: The Sourcebook Project, 2004.

23. Cox, John D., *Climate Crash: Abrupt Climate Change and What it Means for Our Future.* Washington, D.C.: Joseph Henry Press, 2005.

24. Cremo, Michael A. & Richard L. Thompson, *Forbidden Archaeology: The Hidden History of the Human Race.* San Diego, California: Bhaktivedanta Institute, 1993.

25. Darling, David, *Zen Physics: The Science of Death, the Logic of Reincarnation.* NY: Harper Collins, 1996.

26. Donnelly, Ignatius, *Atlantis: The Antediluvian World*. NY & London: Harper & Brothers, 1882.

27. Donnelly, Ignatius, *Ragnarok: The Age of Fire & Gravel*. NY: University Books, 1883/1970.

28. Donovan, Patrick and Herb Joiner-Bey, *The Face of Consciousness: A Guide to Self-Identity and Healing*. Lancaster, OH: Lucky Press, 2006.

29. Dunn, Christopher, *The Giza Power Plant: Technologies of Ancient Egypt*. Santa Fe, New Mexico: Bear & Co.,1998.

30. Dunne, J.W., *An Experiment with Time*. London: Faber & Faber, 1934.

31. Efthyvoulos, Demetri Dimas, *Spirits of the Rainforest: Aspects of the Hyper Real*. Cyprus: 2000.

32. Farley, Gloria, *In Plain Sight: Old World Records in Ancient America*. Columbus, GA: ISAC Press, 1994.

33. Fell, Barry, *America B.C.* NY: Pocket Books, 1976/1989.

34. Fell, Barry, *Bronze Age America*. Boston/Toronto: Little, Brown and Co., 1982.

35. Fell, Barry, *Saga America*. NY: Times Books, 1980.

36. Feuerstein, Georg, Subhash Kak & David Frawley, *In Search of the Cradle of Civilization*. Wheaton, Ill: Quest Books, 1995.

37. Fitzgerald, Astrid, *Being Consciousness Bliss: A Seeker's Guide*. Great Barrington, MA: Lindisfarne Books, 2001.

38. Fox, Hugh, *Gods of the Cataclysm*. NY: Dorset Press, 1976.

39. Freke, Timothy, *Lucid Living*. UK: Books for Burning, Sunwheel Books, Surrey 2005.

40. Gaddis, Vincent H., *American Indian Myths & Mysteries*. NY: Indian Head Books, 1992.

41. Geldard, Richard G., *Remembering Heraclitus*. Great Barrington, MA: Lindisfarne Books, 2000.

42. Girard, Ralph, *Esotericism of the Popol Vuh: The Sacred History of the Quiché Maya*. Pasadena CA: Theosophical Univ. Press, 1979.

43. Goodman, Jeffrey, *American Genesis: The American Indian & the Origins of Modern Man,* New York: Summit Books, 1981.

44. Goodman, Jeffrey, *Psychic Archaeology*. NY: Berkley Medallion, 1977.

45. Goodman, Jeffrey, *The Genesis Mystery*. NY: Times Books, 1983.

46. Gordon, Cyrus H., *Before Columbus — Links between the Old World and Ancient America*. NY: Crown, 1971.

47. Gordon, Cyrus H., *Riddles in History*. NY: Crown, 1974.

48. Gribbin, John & Mary, *Fire on Earth: Doomsday, Dinosaurs & Humankind*. NY: St. Martin's Press, 1996.

49. Hamilton, Edith and Huntington Cairns (eds), *Plato The Collected Dialogues*. Bollingen Series LXXI, Princeton University Press, 1961.

50. Hancock, Graham, *Fingerprints of the Gods: A Quest for the Beginning and the End.* London: Heinemann, 1995.

51. Hancock, Graham & Santha Faiia, *Heaven's Mirror — Quest for a Lost Civilization.* New York: Crown, 1999.

52. Hancock, Graham, *Underworld: Flooded Kingdoms of the Ice Age.* London: Michael Joseph/Penguin, 2002.

53. Hapgood, Charles H., *Maps of the Ancient Sea Kings: Evidence of Advanced Civilization in the Ice Age.* Philadelphia & New York: Chilton Books, 1966.

54. Hapgood, Charles H., *Mystery in Acámbaro.* Kempton, Ill: Adventures Unlimited, 1973/2000.

55. Harris, Hendon M., *The Asiatic Fathers of America.* Published in Taiwan: Undated, late 1970s/early 1980s.

56. Hope, Murry, *Atlantis: Myth or Reality?* London: Penguin Arcana, 1991.

57. Kearsley, Graeme R., *Mayan Genesis: South Asian Myths, Migrations and Iconography in Mesoamerica.* London: Yelsraek, 2001.

58. Kenyon, J. Douglas (ed.), *Forbidden History.* Rochester VT: Bear & Co., 2005.

59. Kovacs, Maureen G. (translator), *The Epic of Gilgamesh.* Stanford CA: Stanford University Press, 1989.

60. Kramer, Samuel, *Sumerian Mythology.* Philadelphia: U. of Pennsylvania Press, 1961/1972.

61. Kuhn, Thomas S., *The Structure of Scientific Revolutions.* Chicago; University of Chicago Press, 1962/70.

62. LaViolette, Paul, *Earth Under Fire*: *Humanity's Survival of the Apocalypse*. Schenectady, NY: Starburst Pubs, 1997.

63. Le Plongeon, Augustus, *Maya/Atlantis*: *Queen Moo and the Egyptian Sphinx*. Blauvelt NY: Rudolf Steiner Publications, 1886/1973.

64. Le Plongeon, Augustus, *Sacred Mysteries Among the Mayas and the Quichés*: *11,500 years ago. Their relation to the sacred mysteries of Egypt, Greece, Chaldea and India*. San Diego CA: Wizards Bookshelf, 1886/1985.

65. Lin Yutang (ed), *The Wisdom of China and India*. NY: Random House, 1942.

66. Lipton, Bruce, *The Biology of Belief*. Santa Rosa, CA: Elite Books, 2005.

67. Little, Gregory L. & Lora H., *The A.R.E.'s Search for Atlantis*. Memphis, Tenn: Eagle Wing, 2003.

68. Little, Lora H., Gregory L. Little & John Van Auken, *Secrets of the Ancient World*. Virginia Beach, VA: A.R.E. Press, 2003.

69. Little, Van Auken & Little, *Ancient South America*. Memphis, Tennessee: Eagle Wing, 2002.

70. Mallery, Arlington H., *The Rediscovery of Lost America*: *The Story of the Pre-Columbian Iron Age in America*. NY: P. Dutton, 1951/1979.

71. McCall, Henrietta, *Mesopotamian Myths*. London: British Museum, 1990.

72. McMoneagle, Joseph, *Mind Trek*. Norfolk VA: Hampton Roads, 1993.

73. Mertz, Henriette, *Pale Ink. Two Ancient Records of Chinese Exploration in America*. Chicago: Swallow Press, 1953/1972.

74. Milton, Richard, *Alternative Science: Challenging the Myths of the Scientific Establishment*. Rochester, VT: Park Street Press, 1994/96.

75. Milton, Richard, *Shattering the Myths of Darwinism*. Rochester, VT: Park Street Press, 1992.

76. Morgan, Elaine, *The Descent of Woman*. NY: Stein & Day, 1972.

77. Morgan, Elaine, *The Aquatic Ape: A Theory of Human Evolution*. London: Souvenir Press, 1982.

78. Morgan, Elaine, *The Scars of Evolution: What our bodies tell us about human origins*. London: Penguin Books, 1990.

79. Muck, Otto, *The Secret of Atlantis*. NY: Time Books, 1978.

80. Nelson, Ralph (translator), *Popol Vuh: the Great Mythological Book of the Ancient Maya*. Boston: Houghton Mifflin, 1974/1976.

81. Nikhilananda, Swami, *The Mandukyopanishad with Gaudapada's Karika and Sankara's Commentary*. Mysore: Sri Ramakrishna Ashrama, 1936/1974.

82. Nityaswarupananda, Swami (translator), *Astavakra Samhita*. Calcutta: Advaita Ashrama, 1940/2001.

83. O'Brien, Christian & Barbara Joy O'Brien, *The Shining Ones*. Cirencester, UK: Dianthus Publishing Ltd., undated.

84. Osborn, Arthur, *The Future is Now: The Significance of Precognition*. NY: University Books, 1961.

85. Santillana de Giorgio & Hertha von Dechend, *Hamlet's Mill: An Essay on Myth and the Frame of Time*. Boston, Mass: David R. Godine, 1969/1983.

86. Schoch, Robert M., & R.A. McNally, *Pyramid Quest: Secrets of the Great Pyramid and the Dawn of Civilization*. NY: Tarcher/Putnam, 2005.

87. Schoch, Robert M., & R.A. McNally, *Voyages of the Pyramid Builders*. NY: Tarcher/Putnam, 2003.

88. Schoch, Robert M., with R.A. McNally, *Voices of the Rocks*. NY: Harmony Books, 1999.

89. Schwaller de Lubicz, R.A., *Sacred Science: The King of Pharaonic Theocracy*. NY: Inner Traditions, 1982.

90. Schwaller de Lubicz, R.A., *The Temple of Man: Apet of the South at Luxor* (2 vols.). Rochester, VT: Inner Traditions, 1998.

91. Sitchin, Zechariah, *Genesis Revisited*. Santa Fe, NM: Bear & Co., 1991.

92. Targ, Russell & Jane Katra, *Miracles of Mind*. Novato CA: New World, 1998.

93. Temple, Robert, *The Crystal Sun*. London: Random House, 2000.

94. Temple, Robert, *The Sirius Mystery*. London: Random House, 1976/1988.

95. Thompson, Gunnar, *American Discovery*. Seattle: Misty Isles Press, 1992.

96. Tolle, Eckhart, *The Power of Now: A Guide to Spiritual Enlightenment*. Novato CA: New World Books & Vancouver BC: Namaste Publishing, 1999.

97. Tolle, Eckhart, *Stillness Speaks*. Novato CA: New World Books & Vancouver BC: Namaste Publishing, 2003.

98. Tolle, Eckhart, *A New Earth: Awakening to Your Life's Purpose*. NY: Dutton, 2005.

99. Tomas, Andrew, *We are not the First*. London: Souvenir Press & Toronto: J.M. Dent, 1971.

100. Tompkins, Peter, *Secrets of the Great Pyramid*. NY: Harper & Row, 1971.

101. Tompkins, Peter, *Mysteries of the Mexican Pyramids*. NY: Harper & Row, 1976/87.

102. Tompkins, Peter, *The Magic of Obelisks*. NY: Harper & Row, 1981.

103. Waddell, W.G., (translator), *Manetho*. London: Loeb Classical Library, Heinemann, 1940/80.

104. West, John Anthony, *Serpent in the Sky: The High Wisdom of Ancient Egypt*. Wheaton, Illinois: Quest Books, 1993.

Resources List for Further Research

In addition to the Bibliography, the authors recommend the following resources for continued study on awakening far memory:

1. *The Monroe Institute*, 365 Roberts Mountain Road, Faber, VA 22938 Tel. 434-361-1252 or 1-866-881-3440. www.monroeinstitute.org

    Robert Monroe developed the renowned *Hemi-Sync*® sound technology and was the founder of *The Monroe Institute*, a respected leader in consciousness research for many decades. Its unique residential programs offer opportunities to explore expanded states of awareness, starting with the *Gateway Voyage*®. There are many graduate courses for further study, including *"Timeline,"* which provides learning adventures designed to gain new perspectives by exploring other selves in other times.

2. *Paul Brunton Philosophic Foundation.* Paul Brunton (1898–1981), a British philosopher and writer, had a major influence on the spread of Eastern mysticism in the West. His writings sum up his view that meditation and the inward quest are not exclusively for monks and hermits, but

also for those living normal, active lives in the Western world. The Paul Brunton Philosophic Foundation is a resource for people who seek deeper experience and broader understanding of themselves, their world, and their Source. www.paulbrunton.org

3. *Eckhart Teachings* (www.eckharttolle.com), supporting the work of spiritual teacher and author Eckhart Tolle, dedicated to the transformation of consciousness and the arising of a more enlightened humanity.

4. *Association for Research and Enlightenment*, based in Virginia Beach, VA, was founded in 1931 by Edgar Cayce (1877–1945) to research and to explore transpersonal subjects such as holistic health, ancient mysteries, spirituality, intuition, philosophy and reincarnation. www.edgarcayce.org

5. *Ancient Wisdom Foundation* is a not-for-profit educational initiative. Its purpose is to further research into the reality of a high and sophisticated civilization existing in remote antiquity (predating ancient Egypt, Sumer and India by millennia) and to communicate the results of that research through print and visual media to a mass audience. www.jawest.net

*"The dream analogy is the key to everything.
If you understand the mechanism of the dream you will
understand waking experience. If we did not have the dream
experience as an example, waking up to Reality might be
almost impossible."*

*Paul Brunton (1898–1981)
(personal conversation, London, October 1948)*

❈ ❈ ❈

*"Once upon a time I dreamt I was a butterfly, fluttering here and
there, to all intents and purposes a butterfly. I was conscious only
of my happiness as a butterfly . . . Soon I awoke and there I was,
veritably myself again. Now I do not know whether I was then a
man dreaming I was a butterfly, or whether I am now a butterfly,
dreaming that I am a man."*

Chuang Tze, 3rd century BCE

❈ ❈ ❈

"Psst! Wake up! You're dreaming!"

Timothy Freke, Lucid Living

About the Authors

John Marett Knowles, M.A. Econ. (Ottawa), Canadian philosopher and parapsychologist, was born in New York in 1923. Pilot and Intelligence Officer, Royal Canadian Air Force (1941–45). A pre-Pearl Harbor American volunteer, he flew "Hurricane" fighters on 146 Squadron, Royal Air Force and was a "Chindit" officer under General Wingate, attached to a British infantry column behind enemy lines in Burma, 1944. He was a post-war, career Public Servant with the Canadian Government (diplomat, consul, trade official) and United Nations (consultant, project manager, senior adviser to governments), serving in many countries worldwide over many years.

A lifelong student of philosophy following a life-transforming mystical experience at the age of eight, his first published philosophical work, *Advanced Concepts of Management,* was written as part of a training program that he designed for trade commissioners of the People's Republic of China and taught in Beijing in 1986. Other philosophical essays have since appeared in appropriate British, American and Cypriot journals. He speaks English, French, German, Italian, Spanish and has a working knowledge of Greek and several other languages.

Linda Anne Leblanc, was born in Ottawa, Canada, in 1953. Beginning in 1977, she accompanied her husband, John Knowles, in his assignments around the world with the United Nations. She also worked in various United Nations organizations in Geneva, Switzerland. She is an accredited Outreach Trainer of The Monroe Institute, facilitating Hemi-Sync® and other workshops. Both a lecturer and a writer, her articles have appeared in magazines and publications in Cyprus and the USA. She speaks English, French and Greek. In December 2006 she was the first foreign-born person of non-Cypriot origin to win public office in Cyprus, when she was elected to the Municipal Council of Peyia, Paphos District. She was also the first woman to be elected to that Council.

Following their retirement to the Eastern Mediterranean island of Cyprus in 1989, they continue to pursue lifelong interests and studies in philosophy, consciousness, the paranormal, including the UFO phenomenon, sacred sites and ancient civilizations. They have attended many residential programs at The Monroe Institute in Virginia and completed the Summer Study Program at the Institute for Parapsychology (Rhine Research Center), Durham, N.C. In 1999, they founded *PSYCHOGNOSIA*, a not-for-profit organization based in Cyprus, for the study and the dissemination of scientifically accurate information on the paranormal.